Saffron Sky

GELAREH ASAYESH

Saffron Sky

A Life between Iran and America

BEACON PRESS · BOSTON

BEACON PRESS
25 Beacon Street
Boston, Massachusetts 02108-2892
www.beacon.org

Beacon Press books are published under the auspices of
the Unitarian Universalist Association of Congregations.

Sections of "The Gulf" appeared in the *Miami Herald,* parts of "Childhood"
in the *Boston Globe,* and part of "Crisis and Connection," "The Dream," and
"The Break" in the *Washington Post.* Variations of the material in "The Return"
also appeared in the *Baltimore Sun.*

05 04 03 02 01 00   8 7 6 5 4 3

This book is printed on acid-free paper that meets the uncoated paper ANSI/NISO
specifications for permanence as revised in 1992.

Text design by Christopher Kuntze
Composition by Wilsted & Taylor Publishing Services

Library of Congress Cataloging-in-Publication Data

Asayesh, Gelareh.
    Saffron sky : a life between Iran and America / by Gelareh
Asayesh.
        p. cm.
    ISBN 0-8070-7210-9 (cloth)
    ISBN 0-8070-7211-7 (pbk.)
    1. Asayesh, Gelareh.   2. Iranian American women Biography.
3. Iranian Americans Biography.   4. Immigrants—United States
Biography.   5. Tehran (Iran) Biography.   6. Chapel Hill (N.C.)
Biography.   7. Saint Petersburg (Fla.) Biography.   I. Title.
E184.I5A8   1999
973'.049155'0092—DC21
    [B]   99-27889

To Homajoon and Baba
and

to Neil

*"I am my beloved's
And my beloved is mine."*

SONG OF SONGS 6:3

Contents

Prologue: The Dream   ix

I. The Return   1

II. Homecoming: America   56

III. Childhood   61

IV. The Break   98

V. The Gulf   114

VI. Homecoming: Iran   132

VII. Fault Lines   166

VIII. Crisis   169

IX. Connection   182

X. In Between   189

Epilogue   216

Acknowledgments   219

Author's Note   222

Prologue: The Dream

Among all the summers of my adult life, there is one that stands out in memory. The year was 1992. Neil and I lived in a white Cape Cod with slate-blue shutters in Silver Spring, Maryland, just outside Washington, D.C. Maple trees, green and feathery, shaded the front yard.

It was a bright, hot summer, unlike any I had ever known before because I spent it at home. I had just quit my newspaper job. My new office was an attic with a skylight, where sunshine filtered through green leaves and dappled the oatmeal carpet. Everyone on our block got up to commute to the city first thing in the morning, leaving me alone with the white cat across the street and the birds in the trees.

For the first time in ten years, I witnessed the mornings ripen into afternoons when the only sound on our street was the whisper of wind rising and falling in the maples. Sitting on the porch with coffee, or walking through the neighborhood on my way to the park or the grocery store, I felt a profound and mysterious peace.

It was not until much later, after the peace had been shattered by a move and the birth of a daughter, that I recognized the secret ingredient of that halcyon summer.

I had achieved, purely by chance, a reincarnation of past happiness. I lived a dream of childhood days in Iran, when activity ceased in the heat of the afternoon sun, and the neighborhood slumbered in silence, and my grandfather's garden filled with the sound of the wind in the apricot trees.

The sun dazzled my eyes. The wind sang to me. The essence of my beginnings rose like sap, infusing my here-and-now with the scents of a childhood Eden. Suspended in illusion, I saw my past melding with my present. The boundaries of space and time were erased. My life felt whole.

I · The Return

Washington National Airport
October 1990

I AM AFRAID. When I say good-bye to Neil, I cling and weep. He is teary-eyed as well. We both feel looming over us the dreadful shadow of the unknown. We hold on to each other as if we might never meet again.

Taking my seat on the plane to New York, where I will board another bound for Vienna, I feel as isolated as if I were on my way to the moon. In Vienna, I will start the last leg of my journey, destination Tehran.

I was born in Tehran. Before my family moved to America, first for a two-year stay when I was eight and then for good in 1977, I was an Iranian girl. Now my country is a mystery to me; shrouded in sinister images. I envision a dark land of ungovernable forces, peopled by bearded bogeymen. It is hard to remember why, in this autumn when war looms in the Persian Gulf, I insisted on going home to Iran.

But two years ago, on a night before my wedding, my aunts called from across the sea to congratulate me. I started to cry and could not stop, although they begged me to, their own voices interrupted by stifled weeping. I was crying over a world in which I could get married without my Khaleh Farah and Khaleh Mina at my side. I was measuring in tears the dimensions of a grief so great that it was unspoken. A detached part of me observed it all, distantly amazed at this well of sorrow that had opened up suddenly at my feet.

So this year, when a green card issued in my name granted me the freedom to travel to and from the United States for the first time since I'd left Iran, I knew what I would do. The decision was organic, flowing unalterably from the grief I acknowledged on that night before my wedding.

I was going back to Iran. I was going to plumb the turbulent depths that overwhelmed me at unexpected moments in a life of surface tranquillity.

I blamed my great fear at the decision on the unknowns of the country I would be visiting. This was convenient, and partly true. But my real terror came from an instinctive awareness that I was beginning a journey into the uncharted regions of my heart.

I did not know what I would discover. I feared what those discoveries would mean for the life I had built here in America.

IN VIENNA my mother, Homa, joins me. Her presence infuses this trip with a comforting camaraderie. The moment she discovered she could not talk me out of going to Iran, Homajoon decided to come along to keep me out of trouble (*joon* or *jan* is an endearment, literally meaning "life," and we have called my mother this for as long as I can remember). My parents share a view of me as heedless and impulsive, so when Homajoon arrives she radiates determination. She plans to shepherd me through the perils of the new Iran. My mother, after all, is the only member of our family who has returned since the revolution. Her last trip was in the heat of the Iran-Iraq war. She told us of trying on shoes in a Tehran boutique as Iraqi missiles landed. As she debated the merits of one pair versus another, the salesman begged her, "Lady, please, make up your mind."

Anecdotes like this have shaped my sense of Iran along with television images that seem alien and frightening, more real to me than the disembodied voices of my family floating out of the telephone earset a few times each year. I live my life in a wholly Western world. My husband, fellow workers, and friends are all American. The only Farsi I have spoken in recent years has been in weekly conversations and periodic visits with my parents and sister, who live in Toronto. The girl I used to be when I left Iran is like an island in an ever-encroaching sea, the victim of fourteen years of erosion. By now, there is little of her left. Yet enough remains for me to have disregarded the possibility of war in the Mideast, and the apprehensions of my family, to seize my chance for a homecoming.

Even my aunts said, "Better not come, Gel-gel jan. It might not be safe." No one can explain to me, using hard facts, why going to Iran might not be safe. For them as for me, the Islamic Republic of Iran is like a dark and murky wood, hung about with a rumor of fear.

Small wonder, then, that when I see the familiar blue and white Iran-Air logo over a deserted desk in the Vienna airport, I feel a chill. I am grateful that we are traveling on Austrian Airlines, where Iran's requirement that women cover their hair does not hold. Even so, joining the other passengers at the gate for our flight to Tehran, we see that most of the women are wearing head scarves. People seem unnaturally hushed. When I laugh out loud at something, Homajoon admonishes me in a whisper: "See, everyone has turned to look at you. Put on your scarf, everyone has put theirs on." I am rebellious by nature, yet I obey after only a moment's hesitation. My docility is a measure of my apprehension and an acknowledgment of the power of the Islamic Republic of Iran to rule me, even halfway across the world.

On the plane, I fasten my seat belt and listen to the conversation taking place behind me, in stilted English, between an Iranian woman and her fellow passenger. She is an English teacher, she says. He is a Portuguese topographer. "This is the first time I go to Iran," the man ventures. "The life there, it's difficult?"

"For women, not for men," the woman responds. "But you cannot drink wine." She pronounces the word "vine," and it takes a few tries for the man to understand. "Ah," he says, subsiding into silence.

A few seats in front of me, a young woman is weeping silently, her shoulders shaking. Her fingers are clenched around a damp tissue, which she presses against the bridge of her nose. When her glance encounters mine, her eyes flick away, staring into space, as if she wants no part of this moment, this plane, its passengers, or its destination. I wonder whom she has been visiting here in Vienna, imagine the airport partings unfolding in her mind's eye, see her counting the months, more likely years, before she will see the ones she loves once again. My mind flits to a cousin who lives near me in Maryland. Bound by immigration restrictions, she has not seen her father for more than a decade. Among Iranians today, such stories are the rule rather than the exception. A father dies, his children wire money from Los Angeles for a headstone that will be erected in a Tehran cemetery. A brother is killed in a car crash; his siblings debate whether it is worth the long trip to attend the funeral. A person once substantial in one's life becomes a voice on the telephone, a signature on a letter, the lesser of two options.

Time and distance, and the futility of railing against either, result in numbness and amnesia. What is ultimately forgotten is one's connection, not only to those left behind, but to oneself as well. This is the immigrant's doom, and this journey to Iran is my attempt to alter it somehow, to fashion for myself a destiny different from that of my peers.

WHEN the plane takes off for Tehran, I feel torn from my moorings, suspended motionless in the sky. My sense of place is annihilated. Time is marked only by the setting sun, the trips to the toilet, the arrival and departure of carts pushed by attractive stewardesses. I study their fresh lipstick and smoothly coiffed hair, stare into the darkness outside my window, exchange desultory comments with Homajoon, eavesdrop on my fellow passengers. The movie comes on, *Pretty Woman.* Julia Roberts's doe eyes and extravagant mouth repeat endlessly on screens throughout the cabin. This airplane hull is a floating fragment of the West, traveling farther and farther east in ever-growing incongruity. As the captain announces our approach to the Islamic Republic of Iran, Richard Gere is untying the prostitute's robe, preparing to make love on the piano. The passengers pore over customs declaration cards, debating whether to disclose their makeup, cassette tapes, and videos—all considered contraband. The stewardesses are now among only a handful of women with bare heads. An announcement comes over the loudspeaker: "Ladies and gentlemen, the import of alcohol and questionable magazines is strictly prohibited. These items must be turned over to us."

On the ground below, the lights of Tehran appear, twinkling in patches. Whole neighborhoods are shrouded in darkness. "Poor saps have oil but no electricity," a man's voice mutters behind me, speaking in Farsi.

A full moon illuminates the night sky. I press my face

against the window, tedium banished. My heart begins to pound.

When the wheels strike the tarmac of Mehrabad International Airport, I am overcome by euphoria. I can scarcely contain myself. Giddy laughter threatens to bubble over when I talk to Homajoon. I cannot believe this moment has come to pass.

But when the slowly moving queue of passengers brings me to the door at last and I step out of the lit shell of the plane into the cool autumn night, my inner tumult is stilled. The harvest moon hangs low over the arid central plain, the *Kavir*. The cool, dry breath of the land caresses my face. Every fiber of my being recognizes it, awakening as if from a long trance.

HOMAJOON nervously fusses with my head scarf, trying to make sure every strand of hair is tucked away as required. On the tarmac, a blue and white Iran-Air bus pulls up and the passengers—the women transformed by scarves and long overcoats and a new reticence—climb aboard. Inside we avoid one another's eyes, as though afraid of acknowledging our hypocrisy. Chewing gum and breath mints mask the fumes of the liquor consumed on the plane. Silence reigns.

The bus stops with a lurch. We walk into a cavernous, empty lounge lit by harsh fluorescence, with empty walls and bare marble floors. Here and there, a green plant relieves the atmosphere of austerity. Gray cubes with navy writing in Farsi and English direct people to the proper lines. It is all cleaner, neater, more orderly than I remember. I stand still for several moments, mesmerized by the sight of computer screens displaying flight information in Farsi. My eyes blur with tears as I stare at the flickering letters. It has been too long since I last saw my innermost self reflected in the world around me.

Rumpled and blinking, standing in line for the first of what will be seven stages of passport and customs clearances, the passengers draw together in renewed camaraderie. "Are my stockings too thin?" a woman wearing sheer hose asks my mother. Officially, only opaque hose is tolerated in Iran. "I put on thick socks in the airplane," Homajoon answers. Then she turns to me: "Don't smile. Don't draw attention to yourself."

The bearded revolutionary guard in the glass cubicle, dressed in green fatigues, takes my passport and checks it against what appears to be lists of names. He hands it back, barely acknowledging my nervous hello, my fervent thank-you. In the customs lounge the bare wall has one ornament, a quote from the Koran in ornate golden Arabic script: "In the name of God, the benevolent and merciful." Nearby hangs a grouping of three photographs, the religious leader Ayatollah Ali Khamenei and the Iranian president Ali-Akbar Hashemi Rafsanjani suspended side by side under an image of the late Ayatollah Ruhollah Khomeini. When I left in 1977, the triumvirate of photos showed the Shah, his wife, Farah, and the crown prince. It is a reminder of who is in charge in modern Iran.

A gaunt, stubble-faced skycap in orange cotton consents to help us with our bags. Moments later, the rumpled customs official in white shirt and dark slacks is glancing from my passport to the pile of luggage teetering on a rusty cart. "I knew a Dr. Asayesh," he says, casually. "He was in the health ministry. He was very well spoken."

"That's my father," I blurt. "He's in Canada now."

The man waves us through without opening a suitcase. Homajoon and I can hardly believe our luck—most passengers are complaining as they hoist one suitcase after another onto the counter to be searched. We walk beaming through the last checkpoint into an overheated hall that is dense with cigarette smoke despite the official no-smoking policy.

Here, official austerity gives way to the welcoming, noisy press of people, a dark, warmly human sea brightened by the colorful clothes of the children and sheaves of red and orange gladioli. My uncle Morteza, my cousin Tooran, other relatives and friends, engulf us. Tears blur into laughter and back again. The faces of the women look subtly unfamiliar. It takes me a while to realize why: they wear almost no makeup.

By the time we wander outside, it is nearly four A.M. Banks of airport lights blaze stark white against a slowly lightening sky. My eager eyes drink in everything: the tiered stands of pines, the neat flowerbeds, the bright yellow signs that designate sex-segregated airport entrances. The scarf draped around my head seems stifling, unnatural. I am longing to take off my raincoat but can't, since it qualifies as my mandatory covering—my *hejab*. So much is new and alien: the taciturn revolutionary guards in their green fatigues, the turbaned images on the walls, the sinister yellow signs ("Sisters' Entrance") hinting at a world of rigidity and restriction.

Yet the cacophony of voices and honking horns around me, the dark mass of the mountains in the distance, the familiar faces and the very feel of the air, speak to me of home. Whatever this land is, whatever I may find here, it is still Iran, and it is a part of me.

MY COUSIN Tooran zips along the deserted streets in an aged Datsun, weighted with as many of our bags as possible. My mother, sitting up front, reaches by habit for the seatbelt. It is broken. "Tooran-jan, this is not safe," Homajoon says. Tooran looks sideways at her and laughs. "We don't have time for those affectations here," she says. A light-colored scarf frames her pale face, the eyes puffy from lack of sleep but nonetheless traced with black liner—little enough makeup that it is overlooked most days by the government minions who police women. Her calf-length jacket doesn't prevent her from expertly shifting gears as she negotiates the early-morning traffic around what used to be Shahyad—Shah Remembrance—Square. It is now called Azadi—Freedom—Square.

In the grayness of approaching dawn, the city seems bleak and ghostly, haunted by ten years of turmoil, hardship, and war. Here and there I see bright yellow signs identifying bomb shelters. Revolutionary slogans cover every wall and overpass. "Death to *badhejabi*" (the inadequate covering of women). "Death to Israel." "God, help us follow the path of Khomeini."

To my companions, the slogans are part of the landscape. "If you find a wall without slogans written on it, let me know," my cousin Reza says wryly. A medical student, he is part of the small contingent of family dispatched by my aunts in Mashad—my family's hometown—to greet us.

Already, America and Neil and my life there seem remote. They are the dream, this is the long-suppressed reality, reborn at last around me. The big news these days is the return of the first prisoners of war from Iraq, the Azadegan or Unconquered Ones. The other topic on everyone's mind is soccer. Iranians' passion for soccer has not diminished since my childhood, when my cousins and I played fierce games on the lawn of our home in Tehran. Now there is nationwide delirium because the Iranian team has reached the finals in the Seoul Asian Games.

A few nights later, Iran wins the championship. The two topics—the Azadegan and soccer—are united when the young players accept their trophy. Their heads are bound in red bands proclaiming "God Is Great." The team captain's speech begins: "In the name of God the benevolent and merciful," and he presents his trophy to the Azadegan and the "martyrs" killed in the eight- year war with Iraq. I look at this display with cynical amusement. The Islamic Republic's propaganda, I am learning, is anything but subtle.

A few weeks later, I am sitting in the darkness of a movie theater far cleaner than the ones I remember from childhood (the Islamic Republic does not allow eating or smoking in movie theaters). A stirring Islamic anthem accompanies the newsreel unfolding on the screen. I am unmoved by the images of marching feet trampling fields of red flowers (the red blooms symbolize bloody martyrdom). I view with detachment the purposeful men jogging to war with red flags waving and the name of God on their lips. They remind me of nothing so much as the footage shown before movies in the Shah's time—but the images projected in those days were of fighter jets and brand-new dams and the rising columns of oil refineries, His Majesty trim in suit and tie overseeing this progress. Though the content is different, the blatant attempt to manipulate the viewer feels the same.

But then the screen fills with footage of the returning prisoners, and within moments I am fighting tears. The stark images follow one upon the other: a man cradling a little girl's black-veiled head and stroking, stroking, stroking, as if he cannot stop. A ragged soldier walking dazed out of an airplane and falling to his knees to kiss the ground. An old woman weeping as her gnarled hands travel across her son's face, as if relearning his features. Here is reality, a deeply human counterpoint to the contrived revolutionary symbolism.

I am stricken with a strange twofold grief, once because of the pain I see captured in those brief images, and once because it is a pain I can never truly share.

AT TOORAN's house in central Tehran, we gather around the kitchen table for an early breakfast: feta cheese, bread fresh from the baker, three or four homemade jams. I eat eagerly, taking in the old familiar tastes, and my cousin Ali jokes: "I guess Gelareh doesn't know that cheese is rationed here in Iran." Later I learn that most day-to-day items—chicken, cooking oil, tea, even automobile tires—are rationed in these postwar years. Lines form instantly when such things go on sale, for though anything and everything can be had on the black market, only the most affluent can afford such prices.

Little by little, other pieces of information assemble, forming a picture of this new-old Iran. The names of streets and familiar haunts have changed—the word "Imam" almost universally replacing the word "Shah." Anything hinting at the West now bears a revolutionary name. The Intercontinental Hotel, for example, has become the Laleh—the Tulip, a symbol of martyrdom in the lexicon of the revolution. Up north, where my family vacationed by the shores of the Caspian Sea, the elite swim on private beaches rather than suffer the indignity of public ones, where a black curtain extends into the sea to separate men from women. In Dizin, a few hours north of Tehran, where I skied as a child, the snowy mountains still draw the affluent, but women take to the slopes wearing knee-length parkas and with their hair covered.

I shake my head, incredulous and disturbed. But things are getting better, my family tells me. The war ended in 1988. With Khomeini's death in 1989 and Rafsanjani's rise to the presidency, there is a gradual easing of postrevolutionary rigidity. In a new movie, the hero is actually shown bare-chested in one scene and touches his estranged wife's hand in another. Dayi Morteza (Dayi means "uncle"), who works for the government-controlled television network, tells me that programmers were recently allowed to reinstate the prerevolutionary tradition of Friday night movies—Friday being the Iranian holiday. The state-controlled radio now permits up to two minutes of popular Western music, including the tunes of

Michael Jackson and Stevie Wonder—instrumental versions
only. Later, driving through the city, Homajoon notices wedding dresses on mannequins in the shop windows. On her last
trip, two years ago, such flaunting of the feminine form was
frowned upon; shoppers had to be content with studying photographs and bolts of fabric.

My family, like most Iranians I meet, seizes on such hints
of change with eagerness. A newly kindled hope provides the
only relief from what seems to be universal frustration over
the hardships and restrictions of daily life. I am taken aback by
the gloom and pessimism that seem to prevail among Iranians
regardless of their political persuasion. The country seems to
be suffering from a collective episode of depression—no surprise given a decade of revolution, war, and economic hardship.

"I should never have returned from France," one friend tells
Homajoon. The last time I saw him was in Paris, on our way to
the United States the year we left Iran. He was a lonely young
student then, homesick for his family. He returned a few years
later. Now, in his forties, married with children, he regrets
that decision. "There isn't one person in this country whose
personality isn't duplicitous, me included," he tells me. "I go
to work, it's 'Yes, sir, your servant, sir, whatever you say, sir.'
When I come home, I'm someone else. I don't know who I am."

Like most Iranians I encounter, our friend seems to vener-
ate the West and everything about it. Our foothold in North
America confers superior status on Homajoon and myself.
The West has always been alluring to Iranians, but now it
seems to possess a glamour commensurate with the decay of
this beleaguered country. In the airport I overhear a grandmother pacify a misbehaving child: "I'll give you chewing
gum. I'll give you foreign chewing gum!"

In Tooran's kitchen we talk for hours, the open window letting in the sounds of streetsweepers and passersby. Eventually the talk shifts to lighter topics. "You have to visit the Carpet Museum," Tooran says. "You won't believe how gorgeous the carpets are. And the Museum of Contemporary Art. And the Museum of Antiquities. A lot of new museums have opened up." By the time Homajoon and I get ready to go to bed, the sun is shining and Tooran's grandchildren, who live downstairs with their mother, are getting ready for school. In the guest room with its accordion door, fresh bedding awaits us on the floor: thick cotton-filled mattresses and quilts, pillows, and the coarse wool blankets I remember from a thousand childhood naps. One side of each blanket and quilt is covered with clean white cotton sheets, stitched or fastened with safety pins. Over the radiator, a wood-framed mirror in the shape of a ship's wheel bears the inscription: SMILING MAKE YOU BEAUTIFUL.

I change into comfortable clothes and lie down, pulling the cool cotton-covered blanket up to my chin, wrapping myself in it like a dear memory. Yet my mind is racing and I cannot sleep.

BY LATE afternoon, we are on our way to the airport again, headed this time for Mashad, a city in the northeast not too far from the former Soviet Union. As we get ready, I notice Tooran's granddaughters glued to the television set. "What are you watching?" I ask. "The Baby Is Mine," the eight-year-old tells me, quoting the title in English. "Who's in it?" I ask. "That blonde woman, the one who replaced Farrah Fawcett on *Charlie's Angels*," she says. I shake my head as I finish putting on my raincoat and scarf. Growing up in the time of the Shah, I wasted my time watching Farrah Fawcett flounce across the television screen. Now, under the mullahs, it's Cheryl Ladd. Some things never change.

My cousin Reza will not be accompanying us to the airport for the hour-and-a-half flight to Mashad. He plans to take the train, and can't be dissuaded, even though he will be traveling all night. When he was in line to pay his train fare, a man gave him money to buy him a ticket as well, and Reza must meet this person at the station. "A stranger trusted you to buy him a ticket?" I ask, incredulous. Reza looks at me strangely. He sees nothing unusual in the incident.

Mashad means "Place of Martyrdom," and it is holy to Iranians because it is the home of the shrine of Imam Reza, the only one of the prophet Mohammad's direct descendants buried in Iran and the namesake of at least three of my cousins along with innumerable other Iranians.

It is holy to me because it is home to my aunts: Khaleh Farah, who became the family elder when my mother left Iran, and Khaleh Mina, who told me stories as a child while I watched the stars on summer nights. My parents both went to school in Mashad, my sister was born there, holidays were spent there. Homajoon and I decided early on in the trip that spending time in Tehran could wait—we must get to Mashad.

But first, we have to pass muster at the Sisters' entrance of Mehrabad airport. Homajoon and I are both wearing pants, so this proves to be no problem. But in a corner of the bleak brown-curtained cubicle, I notice a young woman in a stylish overcoat and bright scarf. Obviously upset, she is scrubbing at her face with a cotton pad. She shows the lipstick-smeared cotton to a dour woman in the government worker's uniform of tunic, pants, and wimple—a head covering similar to those worn by women in the Middle Ages or by nuns. "Can I go in now?" she asks.

"Put on thick hose first," the woman responds, barely glancing up. She uses the familiar form of address reserved for close friends or children.

"Did you see that?" I say to Homajoon as soon as I've left the cubicle. "They treated that woman like a kindergartener." Homajoon nods, resigned and angry. But there is no time to dwell on this troubling facet of the new Iran, for our plane is no more than half an hour behind schedule, and we must say good-bye again. "When you come back to Tehran, I expect you at my house," Tooran tells Homajoon sternly, engulfing each of us in a bone-crushing embrace.

Inside the aging airplane (made in the U.S.), I lean back in a seat upholstered in that pea-green shade so popular in the 1970s, a time when chanting "Death to USA" was tantamount to asking for an introduction to the secret police. Now "Marg bar Amrika" is emblazoned on Tehran walls in garish murals and embedded in neat official script—in English—over the entryways to all major hotels. Public buildings are equipped with prayer rooms, and even lingerie stores display the ubiquitous signs: "We are excused from serving women with inadequate covering." The pilot's rote welcome speech begins with "Peace be upon the pure spirit of the martyrs." A bearded, unsmiling steward makes the rounds with a basket of hard candy. In the newspapers he passes out, I read of three boys whipped for break dancing in a park. Dancing, too, is illegal in Iran.

I put down the newspaper and turn away from my companions. My head is reeling with the contradictions and complexities of my country. My emotions are roiling. As the plane lifts off, I press my face against the window, seeking silence and solitude, longing for a touchstone, an anchor. This feeling is an inarticulate yearning and I do not expect it to be fulfilled. Yet as I take in the barren landscape spreading beneath me, I find solace. In the late-afternoon sunshine, the Iranian plateau is a vast stretch of dun and brown and red, alive with shifting patterns of light and shadow. Ribbed and ridged and naked except

for the light, it gives way on the north and west to mountains
that rise up timeless and majestic, like the very bones of the
earth. In the distance I glimpse Damavand, a lonely peak already dusted with snow. I imagine it looked this way three
thousand years ago, when Aryan tribes first migrated from
central Asia to found the country that would be called Iran,
Land of the Aryans.

I drink in the sight, knowing that this bare earth, uncompromising and immutable, is my foundation. In all those
American years, when Iran came to full consciousness only in
the vulnerable hours of the night, I dreamed not only of the
faces of those I loved but of the land. My hunger for the desert
and mountains and sea was tangible, like a child's longing for
her mother's embrace. We are all a product of our physical geography; it is as if the contours of earth and water and leaf that
fill our eyes during childhood create a corresponding landscape of the mind. It lingers dormant within us, an inner vision seeking completion in outer reality.

I was born on this plateau, this piece of ancient rock cradled
north and south by two seas. Its contours are imprinted upon
my inner eye in a way that time cannot erase. And each time
the windswept spaces of the *Kavir* fill my vision, each time I
see naked mountains, whether in Arizona or Tehran, I feel it, I
feel that sense of completion.

More than an hour later, we approach Mashad in a twilight
illuminated by the rising moon. The emptiness of the *Kavir*
gives way to ordered rows of twinkling lights; Mashad, sheltered from the war by its geography and holy status, clearly
suffers no shortage of electricity. In keeping with tradition, the
plane circles first around the shrine of Imam Reza, the golden
dome and twin minarets breathtaking in their evening brilliance. By the time we reach the airport, night has fallen. Homajoon and I walk the short distance from the shuttle buses to

the terminal quickly, our steps charged with eagerness. A crowd of family is blocking the doorway, a sea of expectant faces. I search for two in particular.

When I feel my aunts' arms close around me, a dam breaks. We hold on tight, weeping silently. But this time the tears are followed by smiles. My cousins, who were mostly in diapers when I left, greet me tentatively. They are young men and women now, yet they wrangle like children over who gets to ride with the two travelers. Several follow me into Khaleh Farah's ancient teal Peugeot, and it is only moments before their diffidence is banished by curiosity. As we ride through crowded streets lined with brightly lit shops I am bombarded with questions about America, which to my cousins seems synonymous with Hollywood. What new films has Steven Spielberg made? Have I heard of the music group Modern Talking? When is *Gone With the Wind II* coming out? Who is more famous, Madonna or Kim Wild?

I have never heard of Kim Wild. She is an actress, I learn. I try to redeem myself by telling them about M. C. Hammer's rap hit "You Can't Touch This." They listen politely. "Reza likes rap," my cousin Soodi offers. Soodi's brother Mammad, it turns out, is a talented break dancer—even though he and his brother Ali were born deaf. Ali is a fan of Madonna, whose posters and music are smuggled into Iran from Kuwait and Dubai and the United Arab Emirates. A brief silence falls, then my cousin Shadi asks Soodi if she has remembered to drop off the book. "What book?" I ask curiously. "*Remembrance.* It's by Danielle Steel," Shadi says. "It's really good." Later, I discover that Steel is a best-seller in Iran as well as in America.

As we drive on, I look at the faces around me in the car, each different and unique. I look at the vibrant life on the streets around me, men and women and children. Sixty million people, all carrying around their own thoughts and dreams. The image in my mind labeled "Iran," built of ignorance and fear and facile suppositions, begins to crumble. In its place, I start to assemble the pieces of a mosaic, colorful and complex, that might more closely approximate the reality of my country.

THE Peugeot turns on a familiar corner. The words I have scribbled for years on airmail envelopes, North Gol Street, take shape on a neat blue sign. *Gol* means "flower," though none is visible. The gray concrete walls that line the street, covered with scribbled messages advertising burglar alarms and plumbers, hide the thirsty gardens and little courtyard pools.

The car pulls up in front of Khaleh Farah's house. I climb out and stand in the dusty, peaceful street under one of the tall, leafy plane trees that cast a welcome shade in daytime. Embedded in the bland facade of the house, the narrow green door I remember stands like a sentinel, its glass block panes giving nothing away. How many times, in dreams, did I arrive on this doorstep, ringing the doorbell, watching a dark shape swim into view behind the distorting glass, ready to grant me entrance?

Each time the threshold remained closed to me, as if in forsaking childhood I had lost the right to enter this house that sheltered me every spring and summer, on family vacations that live on in a remembered blur of noisy mealtimes, peaceful afternoon naps, laughter, and warmth. At lunch or dinner the house was filled with activity, children chasing one another underfoot, men playing backgammon while the women toiled from the kitchen to the table, bearing steaming platters of rice and sauces. Once each trip we would pile into a rented bus to travel four hours to the tiny town of Gonabad, south of Mashad, where my grandfather raised his family and my parents said their wedding vows. We would pick plums and morning

glories in the family orchard at Kalaghabad and try to catch
fish in our hands at the pool in Kalateh, my grandfather's farm.

Our family is scattered now across two continents. The Gonabad house is empty. Kalateh is gone. And the place I called
home in Tehran was razed to the ground years ago.

But here on North Gol Street, at Khaleh Farah's house, time
has stood still.

My cousin Ramin rings the doorbell. A subaqueous form
takes shape behind the glass. Ghamar, Khaleh Farah's servant
for as long as I can remember, opens the door. Her long, narrow
face has thinned since I last saw her. The hair wisping beneath
her scarf and veil is mostly white. But her brown eyes still
slide away from mine as she smiles a wide, glad smile and ut-
ters a flow of mumbled greetings. I embrace her and kiss her on
both cheeks. Her skin is loose and soft and powder dry. I step
across the threshold, taking off my shoes in the stone-tiled
hallway, where a flight of stairs leads to the only room on the
second floor. In the stairwell, a row of African silhouettes
adorn the cream wall, just as they always have. In stockinged
feet, I enter the interior of the house, which lies behind double
swinging doors. It is covered in Persian carpets in rich reds and
blues except for the kitchen and bathroom, where the cold
tiles once again call for shoes—a welter of slippers crowd the
entrance to each area. The boundary between carpet and tile is
still as sharp in my mind as a border crossing staffed with pa-
troling officers. Whenever I violate it by wearing shoes on the
carpet, I tiptoe.

I make a slow, reverent pilgrimage—to the big family room,
where Ramin and I fell asleep night after night in front of the
television set; to the parlor reserved for guests, where I re-
treated as a teenager with my English novels of love and ad-
venture; to the porch with its speckled tiles. The fig tree
and the quince still shade a garden where giant purple asters

and orange marigolds bloom each summer. The tiny stone pool, where Ghamar washes clothes in warm weather, stands chipped and empty. The chicken coop in the corner still holds a few birds.

Back inside, I find the guest bedroom, where my aunt has placed the bed that was mine as a teenager in Tehran. Its wooden headboard has been restored. The Noah's Ark sheets from my childhood, a gift from an American friend, have been stitched onto the quilt that covers the bed. On the walls, I see my own face repeated throughout the stages of my faraway life—the picture that accompanied my first magazine story, Neil and I at our wedding, random family photos I had forgotten sending across the sea. I am delighted at these unsuspected signs of my presence in my family's life, but I feel an aching sadness at our parallel worlds, which until now have intersected so briefly, with snapshots and letters and stilted phone calls.

Yet as Ghamar brings glasses of tea on a tray, Khaleh Farah bustles with preparations for dinner, my mother settles down for a good gossip, and carloads of family fill the house just as they did in all those years long gone. I hang up my raincoat and sink into the familiar green baize armchair in the living room, my heart swelling with gratitude.

THE sun is shining brightly through the drapes when I awake. The sound of a loudspeaker drifts through the open window. At first the amplified male voice sounds threatening, eerie. Then I make out the words: "Sweet pomegranates. Green beans. Fresh spinach. Green beans. Sweet pomegranates."

I lie back, smiling, and let the sound wash over me. I had forgotten the men who make their living with a wheeled cart and a megaphone, peddling onions and fresh herbs, air conditioners and pots and pans, from door to door. I had forgotten the salt-seller, who makes the rounds of the neighborhoods sounding his mournful cry: *Namakiiii.* Each time she hears him call, Ghamar hurries to fetch her well-worn veil and the pile of old bread stored in a corner of the kitchen. She carries it down the steps into the walled backyard and lingers at the garage door, exchanging the bread for rock salt and gossip. The bread, I discover, goes to farmers, who feed it to their cows. I learn early on in my sojourn to save the leftover rice and scraps from our meals for the rooster who crows each dawn from the backyard. In this house, in this country, little is wasted. Partly out of scarcity, partly because of a religious abhorrence of waste, Iranians are natural recyclers, endlessly inventive in prolonging the lives of their cars and clothes and television sets. It was a skill that served my country well in the long years of the war, when the flow of parts and supplies slowed to a trickle. It takes me days to understand why the country seems so faded, so gray: I realize at last that there are no new cars on the roads. Everyone I know is driving the same car they had when I left.

Yet I experience little of hardship in the days that follow. Our visit seems to be one long sequence of feasting, with each relative seeking to outdo the other. In the afternoons, once the daily period for prayer and rest ends between four and five o'clock, a steady flow of visitors come to pay their respects and consume tiny glasses of tea and plates of fruit and nuts and pastries. Around Mashad, the stores stay open past 10 P.M., spilling their bright wares into the street under the light of naked electric bulbs: pyramids of winter melons and pomegranates and tangerines and cucumbers, fragrant bundles of dill and coriander, parsley and mint and basil, stacks of red and white plastic sieves and buckets, gleaming samovars. In the bazaar, the bounty of the land is sold from gunny sacks overflowing with dried figs and peaches, mulberries and raisins, pistachios and barberries, dates and almonds, walnuts and hazelnuts. I don't know the names of half the spices for sale in the

spice sellers' alley, but I'm enchanted by sacks full of dried
flower petals, for use in medicines and drinks and puddings.
The juice stands sell carrot, melon, apple, and pomegranate
juice along with sugary banana concoctions made with milk.
I stand at a busy street corner sipping ruby red pomegranate
juice, and savor the flavor of past autumns, cold and tart and
sweet on my tongue.

I had forgotten the taste. I had forgotten the way men and
women walk about their daily tasks wearing plastic slippers,
easy to kick off when entering the carpeted inner sanctuums
of the home, where shoes are forbidden and prayers are offered
each morning, noon, and night. In a street near Khaleh Mina's
house, young boys string up a volleyball net, interrupting
their game each time a car goes by. In the old quarter near the
shrine, I walk the narrow streets with my mother and aunts
and press against the mud-straw walls to make room for a ragged boy laying his stick against the fatty rumps of several
dusty sheep. Farther on an old blind man stares ahead silently,
allowing his wares—spoons and forks laid out on a piece of
gunnysack—to speak for themselves. Back home on Gol
Street, I watch a man walking home from work, a sheaf of the
long, flat oblongs of bread from the corner bakery folded like
dry cleaning over his arm. A boy in a shirt and loose pajama
pants walks by in the opposite direction, swinging a red plastic
pail in one hand. I know he is taking it to the dairy store to be
filled with yogurt; a staple of every breakfast, lunch, and dinner. My eyes follow the pail as he walks by. It seems to me essential to relearn its features: how the white handle is fitted
into notches in the red sides of the pail.

The taste of pomegranate juice, the sight of sheep on a city
street, the way a pail is made . . . these are the details that define our lives. In forgetting them, I had forgotten my own face.
Here in Mashad, little by little, I am restoring the contours of
my identity.

HERE in Mashad, the sense of coming home is a powerful one. Caught up in the delights of rediscovery, it is easy to believe in fairy tales, that the world I knew in Iran slumbered like Sleeping Beauty's castle, waiting unchanged for the princess to return. My self-absorption delays the inevitable realization that time has marched on, wreaking havoc with people's lives, bringing about divisions that reach into the heart of every family.

This awareness begins with my cousin Ramin's beard. I am not particularly fond of facial hair, but I admire Ramin's, for it complements his lean, hawkish features. I am puzzled when I learn that my family tried to get him to shave in honor of my arrival.

Ramin's beard, it seems, is a symbol. I look at Ramin and I see a handsome young man in the prime of life. My family looks at him, with his dark-rimmed glasses, black beard, and open-necked shirt, and sees a poster child for the Islamic revolution, a reminder of restriction and hardship.

It does not take long for me to discover the beard's corollary among women—the *chador* (the word means "veil" or "tent"). Women in wimples and veils are either devoutly religious or champions of the Islamic Republic —or both. Women who wear scarves over their hair and overcoats called *manteaux* are more Westernized, often resistant to the status quo. These women are interested in fashion, not revolution. They wear a hair clip on top of their head to give their scarves a bonnet-like shape. They follow the prevailing style in *manteaux*. "Last year it was short and tight," a young mother wearing a denim *manteau* tells me over tea and sweets one afternoon. "This year it's long and loose. It depends on the fashions in Europe."

In Iran, there is no middle ground. Each side eagerly seeks converts. "You look so cute in a *chador*," a religious relative of mine says caressingly when I don the veil for a visit to the

Mashad shrine. Mosques usually require veils, some even rent them.

"Wouldn't you prefer a scarf?" an uptown hostess with her hair dyed a gleaming gold asks me, looking with distaste at my functional black wimple. A young relative is less tactful. "I won't be seen with you if you come out in that *chador*," he tells me on an occasion when I choose the veil to allow me greater freedom in what I wear underneath.

New to such distinctions, I tend to choose my mode of dress in accordance with the day's activities (wimples for hiking, head scarves for streetwear, *chadors* for the shrine). I am amused when my male cousins, discussing future mates, establish early on whether or not they want a *chadori* woman. But over time I begin to recognize the passion behind such seemingly innocuous concerns. These distinctions go to the heart of a question that has dominated Iranian politics for most of this century: "Whose country is this?"

During the time of the Shah, Iran was dominated by the secular elite. Today, the mullahs and the devout masses they represent have the upper hand. Iranians all, they seem incapable of finding common ground and regard one another with fear and loathing. "Look at them," a young woman in a purple *manteau* and high-heeled black pumps hisses one afternoon, when I am enduring the interminable line for buying tickets at the government airline office. She motions with her head at three young men who have just walked in wearing army fatigues and beards. "They're revolutionary guards," she tells me. "Just look at those faces. We'd better fix our *hejab*."

"Look at them!" says a middle-age woman at Mehrabad airport a few weeks later, her voice filled with disgust. Her shiny black polyester veil rustles as she turns her back on a group of young women, their bleached curls visible beneath artfully arranged scarves. "They're stepping in his blood," she says.

I turn toward her. A sallow face, settled into permanent lines of discontent, is the only visible part of her body other than her hands. "Whose blood?" I ask.

She looks at me strangely, then reaches beneath the folds of her *chador* and pulls out a wallet. Inside is the black-and-white photograph of a handsome, somber young man. Her son Amir, killed three years ago in the war against Iraq. "I begged him not to go," she says, tears gathering in the corners of her eyes. She knuckles them away. "Wasn't that what this war was about? For us to be an Islamic country, for everyone to wear the *hejab*?"

Her son was twenty when he died. I pat her arm as she searches in her bag for a tissue.

My cousin Ramin went to war. He spent two months at the front and came home stinking to high heaven, his back scored with scratches from crawling through desert scrub. It is Khaleh Farah who tells me this, her capable, careworn hands wiping away the slow tears that trickle down her cheeks. Like the woman in the airport, she vigorously resisted her son's decision to join the army. Ramin's father, Afzal, reacted differently. Afzal, a Mashad University professor best known for his translations of French and English works, including one of Shakespeare's plays, is also a staunch patriot. Honor is more than a word to him. After Saddam Hussein saw his chance to seize coveted territory from a weakened Iran and attacked in 1980, Afzal volunteered for military training. He sent Baba a picture, and I remember how incongruous it looked lying on the glass kitchen table in my parents' apartment in Winnipeg: Afzal and a handful of dusty recruits posed on top of a tank, framed by a drab desert landscape.

Afzal supported Ramin's decision. For days the house echoed with his shouting and Farah's weeping. This was a time in Mashad when, twice a week, bodies came back by the hundreds from the Iraqi front. The air would fill with the sound of keening and cries of "Allah-u-Akbar"—God is Great. Mourning clothes were seldom put away. In the eight years of war, a million people died on both sides of the border.

Two years have passed since the end of the war, and my family does not speak of those days. What I discover of their experiences I learn by chance.

It is a Friday afternoon, and our clan has just finished a lavish lunch. Three big vinyl cloths—the *sofreh*—were spread on the floor in three rooms to accommodate all of us, seated side by side, cross-legged, on the floor. After the meal, the back of the biggest *sofreh* was inscribed, in Ramin's neat script, with the date and cause of this happy occasion: "Homajoon and Gelareh's visit." Now the daughter of the house and her brothers are scrubbing pots in the kitchen while the older guests linger over glasses of tea, passing the bowls of lump sugar and dates back and forth.

In a corner, I see my aunts and mother in conversation with one of Homajoon's old classmates, a woman named Pari. An intensity hangs about them, prompting me to sit nearby. Pari is talking about her remote young son, Hossein, who joined us today at the *sofreh*. He has said little since returning from war a few years ago, his mother confides. "He used to be so full of laughter," she says, weeping quietly into a fold of her white veil. Homajoon's eyes turn red at the corners, her face taking on the look of numb sadness that accompanies unassuageable grief.

In the next room, my cousins are gathering to play parlor games. Joining them, I find Hossein seated a little apart from the group. Laughter alternates with heated arguments as one side consistently loses. Through the noise, I become aware of Ramin's low voice as he sits next to the silent Hossein. "I lost three buddies," Ramin is saying.

I realize he is talking about the war. Ramin's face shows nothing but genial good humor, his eyes gleaming behind his glasses, one knee drawn up before him to support his bent arm. "Lots of the guys were killed," he tells Hossein. "One of them—a shell hit his shelter directly. He was reduced to powder."

Hossein, coming out of his trance, seems to listen closely.

"He was from Shahrood," Ramin adds, like an epitaph.

The two are silent, their eyes seemingly fixed on the same distant scene. Around them the game continues, the players oblivious of the conversation in the corner. Then Ramin says with a sort of wonder, "The bullets sounded just like the buzzing of bees."

Someone calls my name, and I turn my attention back to the game. But my eyes stray often to Ramin, searching to divine the essence behind a face I have known all my life. At twenty-seven, Ramin is only a year younger than I. Yet he seems as young to me today as he did in the days that he followed me around Khaleh Farah's house, proposing one playful enterprise after another. Once, he suggested we boil potatoes for a private snack. He had this idea just before lunch, which was to be held that day at Khaleh Mina's house. The two of us carried the hot potatoes in plastic bags, and they banged against our knees as we skipped and ran through the sunny streets to our aunt's house, laughing all the way. We hid in a corner, out of sight of the women carrying laden trays to the *sofreh*, and ate them out of the bag, which was filmed with steam. By the time they called us to lunch, our appetites were gone, but we thought those potatoes the most delicious we had ever eaten.

Today, Ramin is as sweet-natured, as quick-tempered, as maddeningly impractical as ever. He still likes to fiddle with radios. He still drives his parents crazy with his ability to argue some minor issue to the death. He still falls asleep at night in front of the television set, mouth slightly open, snoring gently, with every light in the house burning.

But he has been places I can never go, become a person that I can't really know.

THE days fall into a certain rhythm, each week culminating with a family gathering on Friday, the Iranian weekend. This week, we pile into battered cars and drive into the hills just outside the city. We hike for an hour before stopping at a tree-shaded restaurant in the village of Shandiz. My cousins take me there to sample Shandiz's famous *shish-lik*—mouth-watering rack of lamb on metal skewers grilled on a charcoal brazier.

We sit at a long table, the flowered vinyl tablecloth covered with a sheet of plastic. A box of Kleenex makes do for napkins. A waiter in an open-necked white shirt and dark slacks brings icy colas and a pitcher of *doogh*, the mint and yogurt drink traditionally served with kabab. We swat at the bees while we wait. Side dishes arrive: bread hot from the oven, plates of fresh herbs and raw onions, big tin platters of yogurt. The yogurt, sweet and tart, is the best I've tasted in decades. I try to concentrate on the taste, ignoring the annoyance of eating with a scarf over my head. The scarf still seems like outerwear to me, as awkward as eating with my mittens on. But the meal, when it comes, more than makes up for the discomfort of restaurant eating in Islamic Iran. The lamb is still smoky from the brazier, the rice glistening with butter and crowned with red-gold saffron.

Outside the dining room, a fountain sprays bright droplets into the dry air and families lunch in traditional style. Instead of tables and chairs, wooden platform beds covered with Persian carpets sit under the trees. The carpets look cheap, but they are thick and richly colored. After lunch, the *sofreh* is cleared away and the bed is devoted to another purpose: people stretch out for a doze or linger for hours over small glasses of tea and polished wooden backgammon sets while the birds sing and the light fades in the sky.

We leave the restaurant to drive farther into the country, my younger cousins singing and urging whoever is driving to pass the car ahead. The road winds through stands of trees turned gold and red, blending into dun-colored hills that slope gently upward into a deep blue sky. A small river, scarcely more than a stream, rushes over stones below. Eventually we stop at a café built precariously on the riverbank. My cousin Ali orders their very best tea, and as the wizened old woman who runs the place fires up her samovar, we clamber down the bank to the rushing stream. The smell of water mingles subtly with the smell of dust. Platform beds are strategically placed to catch the cooling breezes, one straddling the stream. The wind whispers in the trees, the sound of rushing water soothes and beguiles, and the tea, when it arrives, is hot and strong enough to make one's mouth pucker. We pass the bowl of lump sugar back and forth, talking idly. One of my cousins stretches out for a nap. It's near sunset, when the *mu'azzin* will issue his call to prayer, and one of the older women squats by the stream to unroll her thick gray stockings beneath her veil. I catch a glimpse of her calf, white flesh that has rarely seen the sun. She scoops water from the stream to perform the ablutions required before *namaz*—the Muslim prayer—washing face and arms and feet in a sequence dictated by religion. My great-uncle, who has already washed, climbs onto one of the carpeted platform beds, unselfconsciously bending and straightening in prayer. The sky and the trees frame his tall, lean body as he holds his hands in front in ritual supplication. The rest of us, those who don't pray or put off praying until the last moment, lounge on the beds, sipping tea. Reza asks for the sugar bowl. My cousin Soodi is giggling over something Maryam has said.

Drinking in the peace of this moment, I feel a pang of envy for the ability my countrymen seem to have to savor, rather than take charge of, life.

NOT long after our country outing, on a cold autumn night, Khaleh Farah takes me to the Shrine of Imam Reza. She wants me to make my pilgrimage, as a good Muslim is required to do on entering the city, but I sense a deeper purpose. Khaleh Farah's low-heeled shoes click across the vast tiled courtyards in a characteristically staccato pace. We head for the main section of the shrine, the courtyard surrounding the Imam's tomb. "This is a holy place," my *khaleh* is saying as we walk. She is slightly out of breath, her eyes wide and serious. "Every verse of *namaz* spoken here has the value of a hundred thousand spoken anywhere else. The same with regular prayers. This is a corner of heaven, you see."

In this corner of heaven, as in any place devoted to prayer, shoes are forbidden. At the entrance to the great mosque, we slip our shoes into a plastic bag and walk across the threshold, blending at once into the jostling crowds within. The glittering mirrored halls are ablaze with electric light, heated by the press of human bodies. The cool marble is smooth beneath my stockinged feet. Khaleh Fareh makes her way to a corner, finding a *mohr*—the prayer stone—on the shelves by the window. I watch my aunt pray, her eyes fixed on a place I cannot see, her face still except for the movement of her lips. I go through the motions of prayer as best I can, feeling awkward but strangely content. After so many years away, just being near my aunt brings me a deep sense of peace. When she is done, we leave as briskly as we arrived.

In the chill of the outer courtyard, we walk to the open gates that lead to the street. Khaleh Farah pauses at the final threshold. She turns back to face the golden dome, the twin minarets, and bows deeply. When she straightens, the distant glow of electric light illuminates the tears tracking down her cheeks. Her fingers are squeezing mine painfully. "Thank you very much, Master," she says. "Thank you *very* much."

I say nothing but squeeze her fingers in return, at last understanding our purpose in coming here. The Imam has brought me back to her, and she has come to offer up her gratitude. Between us hangs a shared awareness of the miracle of this moment in time that has us standing hand in hand.

Her fingers in mine are firm and warm and real. I bow my head, making my own obeisance to the light.

LATER, I remember with humor and a certain delight my aunt's mathematical equations about the superior value of prayers uttered in the shrine. It is the kind of amusement you might feel when a child explains, in all earnestness, why the earth is flat. Even so, long after that night I am haunted by the look on my aunt's face as she offered me her truths.

It takes me years to understand why. I realize at last that her eyes and voice were full of the kind of reverence I haven't felt since I was a child. Living in America, with its lofty intellectualism, has robbed me of simple faith, that precious legacy of growing up in a simple land. I realize the essential magic of belief, that its transformative power lies not in *what* you believe but *that* you believe. I begin to see that it is our capacity for awe that links us to the divine.

Even in America people want to believe—in Santa Claus, in angels, in the Chicago Cubs.

I grieve for my loss. I want my capacity for faith restored. I want to believe in miracles.

But I feel deflowered, incapable of recapturing a lost innocence.

IN KHALEH Farah's guest parlor, our visitors sit side by side on the dark blue velvet loveseat. Zivar, a slender, stylish woman in her late forties, has two grown sons as well as the mischievous preschooler now hiding behind her skirt. Her hair, dyed a deep honey, frames a dark and vivid face. Her husband, Mr. Ahmadi, is a vigorous man with a trim mustache. Our conversation begins along the expected lines, warm superficialities exchanged over tea and fruit and pastries for the half-hour required by protocol.

But along the way we hit a treacherous shoal—the scandalous venture of Zivar's brother into bigamy. We shake our heads as we discuss the Islamic regime's revival of this practice, which was illegal under the Shah. The brother has been married to his first wife for twenty years, but the marriage, always turbulent, included frequent separations. During the most recent one, he met someone. "I told Maliheh"—Zivar says of her teenage niece—"'Don't leave your father alone so much.'" She lowers her voice and bends toward us. "She was out all the time, he felt neglected . . . You see what happened."

I think of Zivar's brother, a handsome, well-to-do man in his early fifties. "He's a grown man," I say. "He should know better."

Zivar nods, but her husband, largely silent until now, speaks up. "Men have special needs," he says. "Women have to take care of their men. If a man has a need, a shortfall in his life, and he sees that his buddy has four wives, well . . ."

The four women in the room, Homajoon and I, my aunt and his wife, stare at him silently. My mother looks incredulous. His voice trails off and he looks away, but his mouth sets in stubborn lines. Zivar shakes her head and looks at me. "Iranian men," she says. "You see what Iranian men are like, Gelareh-jan?"

"My father is Iranian," I respond, ignoring my mother's frantic eyebrow messages. "He's not like that."

Homajoon and Khaleh Farah rush into speech to smooth over my breach of etiquette, but when the couple rise some moments later to take their leave, Mr. Ahmadi is less than cordial.

MY FRIEND Nargis tells me this story. She is standing at a street corner, waiting for a cab to take her to the hospital where she works as a psychologist. A self-important woman from the *komiteh*, one of the committees that rove the streets policing public morals, accosts her. She is swathed in black and young enough to be Nargis's daughter. "Lady, your hair is showing," she says. "I need you to come in for questioning."

"I told her, 'These four strands of hair you see here have looked just like this since the revolution,'" Nargis says, gesturing with manicured nails to the bronzed bangs that fall over her forehead. "I said, 'I'm on my way to the psychiatric ward of XYZ hospital right now, I don't have time to come for questioning. If you want, you can always get an appointment with me there.'" By the time the delicate insult had sunk in, Nargis had hailed a cab and was on her way.

Nargis is smiling. Her friend Roohi and I laugh, delighted with the story. We sit around the kitchen table in Roohi's luxurious Tehran apartment, sharing tea and solidarity.

"HE told me, 'Wait until you see her,'" says Manijeh, her delicate face lined with age, her eyes hidden behind large, smoky spectacles. She mimicks her husband's cajoling tone. "'She's so pretty,' he said."

Manijeh looks across the table at Homajoon. My mother doesn't know what to say; shock and pity show on her face.

"So I got my things and left."

Manijeh's daughter, Parvin, shakes her head. Parvin now shares this comfortable house in North Tehran with her mother, her daughter, and the daughter's husband and two children. "You see what Maman has done?" she says to Homajoon. "She has left all her things, her life, for that woman to take over. I told her she should stay."

I look at Parvin incredulously. Manijeh shrugs hunched shoulders in a dismissive gesture. But her lips are trembling.

NOTICE in a houseware store in Isfahan:

Know sister that the value of a woman lies in her purity and honor and the hejab *is the golden key to those virtues, so never lose your* hejab. *Brother, a glance is a poisoned barb from the devil and well it may be that one glance brings long regret in suit.*

SLOGAN on a wall in Mashad:

Badhejabi *is a form of psychological complex.*

POSTER on an airport wall:

"Good." [Under an image of a woman wearing a calf-length coat, slacks, and a gently draped scarf that shows only the round moon of her face.]
"Better." [Under the image of a woman wearing a wimple and all-enveloping chador.]

Both women are faceless.

ENCOUNTER at Mehrabad International Airport.

"Your hose are too thin," the surly sister on duty says to me. "Put on thick ones, then you can come in."

"But I don't have any!" I complain. "I have to meet my friend's plane. She's waiting for me."

The sister shrugs and looks away. My friend Mahtab has the same problem, but, more experienced than I, she keeps an extra pair of stockings in her purse. She puts them on and is waved through. "Wait for me outside," Mahtab says.

I leave the building, mortified. The chill air does not cool my temper nor soothe my sense of impotence. A foiled attempt to enter through another door, manned by a revolutionary guard who regards me with careless curiosity, makes me feel worse. I sit on the low wall just beyond the entrance, kicking my heels against the rough stone.

Suddenly a familiar face emerges from the crowd outside the airport. It is Mahtab's driver. Surreptitiously, he hands me a wadded-up ball of black material and leaves. I put on my friend's spare stockings gleefully. The sour-faced sister glances through my purse and lets me in. Once inside, I take off the stockings and hand them back to Mahtab. This small act of rebellion does wonders for my morale.

As I wander through the arrivals hall, taking note of the many women whose sheer stockings reveal their mastery of the system, I begin to feel positively smug. Yet the experience has hardened me, creating a new understanding of the simmering resentment that characterizes so many Iranian women.

A few days later, I take a cab into the city to interview someone for a newspaper story. It has to be a cab licensed to enter the Tarh, the area restricted by Tehran's traffic plan. (Traffic in this city of about fourteen million is so bad that for much of each weekday, only cars with authorized business are permitted downtown.)

I finish early and decide to drop in on a relative who works in a government ministry. The cab lets me off at the corner, and I walk up shallow marble steps to the large modern building. The women's entrance is policed by a matronly sister who sits, clearly bored, behind a glass partition. She asks to see my identification and lingers over my U.S. driver's license, her eyes filling with a curiosity akin to warmth.

I wait for the kinds of questions I've become accustomed to: "Is life good there?" "Why would you come back?" "Are the men good husbands?" I assume a friendly, expansive expression, confident that my link with the privileged West will carry me easily over this hurdle.

The woman asks no questions. Instead, she peers closely at my face, finds what she's looking for, and tells me I can enter—once I've taken off my eyeliner.

I am flabbergasted. The tiny hint of liner I occasionally wear is virtually invisible, especially compared to what most Iranian women consider makeup.

Then I see the subtle satisfaction on her face and I understand. I may have money and freedom and status beyond her reach, but she has authority. Khomeini's revolution was about empowering the masses at the expense of the privileged. I feel as if I have experienced one of the ways in which this promise has come true.

I take back my driver's license, scrub at my eyes with a tissue, and march off in a rage. Much later, I cannot decide which is more pathetic, her petty tyranny or my sense of entitlement.

IT IS late at night. Our old friend Bijan is driving through Tajrish Square on the way home from a party, Homajoon and I sitting in the back. Bijan's wife sits in the front, but sideways so as to not commit the solecism of turning her back on Homajoon. The conversation flows easily as we trade the hustle and bustle of the square for an empty, shadowed street. Suddenly a roadblock looms out of the darkness.

Three youths in army fatigues, one armed with a G3 rifle, wave our car to a halt. They are Basijis, members of the volunteer militia characterized by its religious zeal and lack of discipline.

A young boy with close-cropped hair shines a flashlight inside the car for a moment, then steps back. It is not clear what he is looking for, and we are not about to ask. There is something about the boy's face that suggests a frightening awareness of his own power. Or perhaps it is I who am all too aware of my own powerlessness.

The boy waves us on. Bijan puts the car in gear. On the way home we are silent. As I watch the quiet streets flash by, I cannot decide if I have just experienced a brush with danger. Would the right combination of events, a chance spark, have ignited something that could rage out of control?

None of us knows for sure. It is not until we are home, surrounded by bright lights and familiar things, that the sense of normalcy trembling on the edge of nightmare recedes.

I HAD ARRANGED to be in Tehran on November 4, the anniversary of the taking of the U.S. hostages. Here they call it the Eradication of the U.S. Den of Spies. I go as something of a curiosity-seeker, tagging along with a friend.

We arrive at the street in front of the former U.S. Embassy, now a school for revolutionary guards, to find a holiday atmosphere. Excited schoolgirls laugh and chatter, wearing red headbands with the message "Death to America." A man on a truck, armed with a megaphone, exhorts the crowd to take up the same chant. "Marg bar Amrika! Marg bar Amrika!"

Men and women gather in separate sections. Too late, I recognize my mistake in wearing my black *manteau* and a loosely draped scarf. I am the only unveiled woman for as far as the eye can see.

My friend Mazyar wades through the men's section in search of a better vantage point. I follow close behind, listening to the men mutter angrily that a woman—an unveiled woman at that—is in their midst. Mazyar pretends not to hear. They scrutinize his hazel eyes, light skin, and bomber jacket and conclude, wrongly, that he is a foreigner. "Khare-ji-eh," they mutter to one another. "Let him go." I keep my head down, avoiding the hostile glances that follow me.

Once we reach our goal, I hand Mazyar my camera and ask him to take photos for me. Eager to avoid more attention, I head for the women's section. Posters and banners wave unsteadily above the crowd, one depicting footprints tracking across the U.S. flag, another a squint-eyed effigy of Uncle Sam. Atop the wall of the former embassy, men are clustered around the microphone. The master of ceremonies is an unassuming man in glasses. The expected stubble—to be clean-shaven here is to be excessively Western—shadows his dark skin. "First we'll have some slogans," he tells the crowd. "Then we'll hear the declaration. Then we'll burn the U.S. flag."

I am smirking at the absurd agenda when a flock of *chadori* women with "Security" pinned on their sleeves descend upon me. "Lady, your *hejab* is greatly lacking," one says. "You can't go until you fix it." She tugs at my scarf, frowning. "First pull this down so that no hair is showing."

"Button up her collar," another women says. A second set of hands tugs at my lapels in an attempt to cover the white V of the T-shirt showing beneath my *manteau*. I submit demurely, feeling tension but no fear, for their demeanor is at once reproving and subtly maternal. They are clearly enjoying themselves. When they are done with me, I sit down on the asphalt.

Speakers follow one after the other, but I pay little attention, distracted by a low conversation in the row behind me.

Two young girls swathed in black argue earnestly about the importance of unity in the Islamic movement. "But why should there be so many different factions?" one is saying. Before I can hear more, we hear a distant hubbub. The people around me prick their ears. Someone speculates that a rival faction is trying to disrupt the demonstration.

Nothing happens. The speeches are over, the microphones are dismantled, the crowd begins to disperse. I set off in search of Mazyar, who hands me back my camera. We head for the car and lunch.

As I step across asphalt littered with leaflets, I am overcome with a sense of unreality, as if I have just participated in a game of charades.

I RETURN to the streets around the U.S. Embassy a few weeks later for a dinner party. The daughter of the house offers the guests tea and fruit, then comes to sit beside me on the couch. Before long we are talking about mutual acquaintances, many former classmates of mine from Iran-Suisse academy, a Tehran private school. Most are abroad, she tells me. A few live in Tehran still, married, with families.

Reza K. lives in London. He visited a couple of years ago.

Elham spent four and a half years in prison. A wholehearted convert to the Islamic regime, she is now in medical school.

Kourosh disappeared. "We think he was smuggled out."

Shahriyar's trial was televised. He was a hostage for his father, who was suspected of participating in an attempted coup. "He kept on saying, 'I didn't know anything,'" my friend tells me. I imagine his bold face, grainy and fear-washed on a television screen.

He was nineteen when they executed him.

WHEN Shahriyar was thirteen, our classrooms were on the second floor in Iran-Suisse's old wing, overlooking Kakh Avenue. He liked to sit in the back. I sat up front, next to the big windows, where I could stare out at the trees and sky. In spring, the leaves were a new green, infused with light against a blue backdrop. In winter, the bare white bark of the branches was limned against a sky pale and heavy with the promise of snow. The sounds of traffic below drifted up, muted, to my window. Those sounds belonged to the outside world while my classmates and I were sheltered within the walls that encircled our school.

Even more than these brick barriers, our sanguine confidence sheltered us. We knew beyond a doubt that it was what happened among us—dodgeball in the afternoons, the annual Christmas party in English class, dancing daringly cheek to cheek at birthday parties where the boys dimmed the lights—that really mattered. It never occurred to us to think of ourselves as children or of the outside world as one shaped by forces beyond our ken.

When the school year ended, our headmistress decided to make Iran-Suisse a primary school. She closed the upper grades, and our small universe shattered. My friends and I scattered. Even so, when I left Iran, it was my classmates from Iran-Suisse to whom I wrote. At first I would start the letter with a date from the Iranian calender: First of Esfand, 1356. Soon I lost track of the Iranian days, then the months, then the years. Swept up in a world bigger than any I had imagined, the life I had known became first remote, then irrelevant. The names of my old friends became relics from another age. I heard that Ali was in Canada, Shahrzad in England, Azadeh in Switzerland. I kept in touch with Steve in California, discovered Babak by accident in North Carolina, and Bahram in Delaware.

For years I received regular letters with a Tehran postmark from Kourosh. In his tiny, even script, my friend would describe the city of my birth under a blackout, reduced to a ghost town by the threat of Iraqi missiles. But I did not know how to respond. By the time I figured it out, the letters had stopped. Kourosh was gone.

When my friend Elham was jailed for her membership in the People's Mujahedeen, an Islamo-Marxist group responsible for much of the violence against Iran's clerical leaders, I could not fathom the dimensions of her fate.

When I heard that Shahriyar was dead, I went to a secluded spot on the campus of the University of North Carolina at Chapel Hill to mourn. But my thoughts kept returning to how I would tell my American classmates, to the special, tragic cachet of knowing someone who has been executed. My tears were horribly tainted.

I felt my own shallowness yet was helpless to change it, for just beneath lurked a great void, empty of all feeling.

I BRAVE the torrent of city traffic one day to visit the vast cemetery in South Tehran, Behesht-e-Zahra, or Zahra's Heaven. At the entrance, a giant pair of hands holds aloft a red tulip. Through the haze of gasoline fumes, the dome and minarets of the hastily erected tomb of Ayatollah Khomeini glint a dull gold.

In the newer section of the cemetery, I walk among a forest of aluminum spires adorned with the red, green, and white Iranian flag, plastic flower bunches, wilting gladiolas. Each set of spires frames a metal cabinet. Inside, the faces of young men killed in the war with Iraq are locked away behind glass, along with fragments of lives now stilled: photographs, childhood mementos, figurines from a wedding cake. On marble headstones, flowery verse hails these martyrs. "From the battlefront comes the chant of 'Our lord,'" reads one. "'. . . Open the gates of heaven!'"

Not far from the forest of spires, the sun beats down on a rocky plot of land bare of tombstones or tokens of love and remembrance. "This is where the *ma'doomin* are buried," my friend Hassan tells me in a low voice. He ducks his head in a strangely furtive gesture and turns away. "Best not to linger here."

The *ma'doomin*.

The executed.

I wonder if one of our number lies here, one of the thirteen-year-olds who saw the future stretching out before him as an endlessly bright horizon.

I stand there for a long moment after Hassan moves on, just in case.

ONE night, years after my visit to the plot where he might be buried, I lie in bed thinking of Shahriyar. In my mind's eye, I conjure him up as he was before he left the magic circle of our schoolyard. I see his arrogance, his habitual smirk. I see his eyes, dark and knowing under the too-long fringe of straight bronze hair. His hair flapped behind him when he walked, each step surging with restless energy, the steps of a boy hurrying toward manhood.

His name, Shahriyar-e-Noor, meant King of Light. He was the king of a band of semirenegade boys who lounged in a shady corner of the schoolyard, ogling the girls and pushing the narrow boundaries of what we considered propriety.

He rode motorcycles on the weekends. His wealthy father ran a club where glamorous and cynical men and women gambled. He once got a windbreaker from England and wore it constantly, insisting that it was so well made he could be comfortable in all temperatures.

Once, a weeping girl went to him with the story of how another boy had kissed her without permission ("He *kissed* her!" the rest of the us whispered in shock tinged with envy.) Shahriyar placed his British windbreaker protectively around her shoulders, then went to confront the culprit.

How worldly he seemed to me then. And yet he was inno-
cent, oblivious of his own mortality.

The sound of rain fills the darkness outside my window.
I imagine it falling on the pines, sinking into the green grasses,
soaking the sandy Florida soil. My mind is filled with the image of a merciless sun beating down on a barren plot of earth.
Tears flow.

I do not deserve the rain.

Gonabad
November 1990

I BEND my head to pass under the old doorway, walking
through the dim corridor and into the courtyard. My eyes
are momentarily blinded by the sun.

When I can see again, I stand still for long moments, taking
in the ruin of my grandfather's garden. I came to Iran thinking
I could change the course of decline and diaspora and distance.
Now I see, all around me, the full evidence of the relentlessnes
of time. My American illusions (anything is possible) crumble
under the blue Iranian sky.

"I've been saying we should sell the place," Dayi Morteza
says, coming up beside me. "Or tear it down and build anew."

I turn away, unable to answer. Beneath my feet, the autumn
leaves rustle on dusty flagstones. The trees are an overgrown
tangle of gold and brown and green, with touches of vermilion
where pomegranates have withered on the branch. The old
apricot trees gave out years ago.

An old ladder leans against the mud wall, which has tumbled down in sections. Bees hum and zing through the clear
autumn air. Everything has an aura of silent waiting, of quies-
cent emptiness—the mud bricks, the blue sky, the pomegranates suspended motionless from their branches. The old house

hunkers in the sun, dreaming old dreams of children grown and scattered, of a mother and father gone to their graves, of births and weddings and family squabbles.

I walk slowly across the courtyard. The blue pump is broken. When I open the trap door, I see that the cistern has dried up, choked now with refuse. Nearby, wooden crates brim with pomegranates that have withered awaiting transport to Mashad. I walk past the empty stone pool, littered with leaves and rotting fruit, to stand in front of the avenue I remember. Once it was a wide stone path, shaded by neat almond bushes, running straight and true from the house at one end of the garden to my grandfather's office at the other end. Now it is thick with dust and dry leaves, the boundaries obscured by weeds.

At the other end of the garden, where once an old man sat with his clean, dry physician's hands resting on a wooden desk, the three rooms are dark and derelict. Spider webs trail over the faded posters from pharmaceutical companies. The mud oven next door has not been fired in years.

I walk back through the trees, which weep soft whispering dust onto my head and shoulders each time I brush against them. At the end of the avenue, I stand for a moment, looking at the graceful, whitewashed facade of the old house, every curve and arch echoing deeply in memory. I am driven to visit each special place, needing to know what has become of it. The spiral staircase leading up to the roof is impassable, blocked with broken masonry and garbage. Beneath the iron trap door to the basement, only dirt and scorpions linger. In the atrium room, the carpeted window seat where I read my English novels as a child is bare and thick with dust, the pink gauze curtains limp and tattered. I look at the familiar snowscape on the ledge, at two old chairs, upholstered in burgundy and cream, now showing their springs.

In the large central room I slide down against the cold wall, pull up my knees, close my eyes against the sight of the mustard carpet remnant that covers the floor, and bury my head in my arms. I travel backward in time to the days when these rooms were peopled, the floors covered with bright carpets, the kitchen wafting savory smells, and servants bustling across the courtyard with their tea trays. I travel forward in time to a future when the few whose love still tends this overgrown garden will be gone.

"Don't cry, Gel-Geljan," Khaleh Mina says, laying a hand on my shoulders. "I know, it's terrible. I want to cry too when I come here."

Khaleh Farah watches me in abject misery, as if she were to blame for what I see around me. "I'm sorry it's so rundown," she mutters, brushing a tear from the corner of one eye. "We do what we can, but it's difficult."

I raise my head, realizing my selfishness. "You've done a wonderful job," I tell her fiercely, knowing that it is Khaleh Farah who has been burdened with the upkeep of this house for all these years. "If it weren't for you, this would all be gone."

We sit together in silence. In the courtyard, the rest of the family is getting busy. Giti-jan, who was my mother's age when she married Homajoun's uncle, wields a broom in one corner, sweeping away the dead leaves. Ramin follows in her wake with a hose, sending a jet of water onto the tiles. Giti-jan's son Hamed is dispatched to the baker for bread. Ali, at twenty-eight the oldest of my Iranian cousins and used to responsibility, has unearthed the *mashk*—a plastic container that reaches above his knee. It bumps against his leg as he strides off to fetch clean water from the city cistern a few blocks away; my aunts trust the tap water here only for washing.

My cousin Maryam, armed with broom and hose, her pants rolled up above the ankles, attacks the *hammam*, the new bathhouse with a toilet adjoining a tiled room fitted with faucets and a shower. Khaleh Farah had the *hammam* built in anticipation of my trip so we wouldn't have to use the public baths in town. Now my aunt covers her mouth with a cloth, finds another broom, and sets to sweeping the dust from the rooms. Little by little, the abandoned garden comes alive, and with it my optimism.

I will not relinquish the past. I will hold on to what I can for as long as I can.

I tie my scarf over my mouth and go to take the broom from Khaleh Farah.

WHEN Afzal arrives later that afternoon, he tells me that tomorrow we will visit the "well of Mr. Nobari." We set out the next day, driving through rutted tracks for fifteen minutes until we arrive at a large, still pool that gleams in the sunlight next to a small hut. Just beyond the pool, a clear stream rushes across waving green algae. It is lined by a row of tall evergreens that march across the open fields like sentinels. This is where Mr. Nobari and his wife, originally from Mashad, live when they are supervising workers in the fields where saffron, pistachio, broom, and barberry grow. The pool feeds them all, filling up overnight with water pumped from the well and emptying into irrigation canals each day.

Mr. Nobari, a lanky, sunburned farmer wearing a gray wool hat, comes out to greet us, wringing Afzal's hand warmly. In the little hut there is a single bed, a thick Persian carpet, cushions propped against the wall, and a samovar. We settle down on the carpet, cushions at our back, as Mrs. Nobari dispenses hot tea and brings Afzal up to date on her family.

Mrs. Nobari goes on to talk about the saffron harvest, which consumes much of southern Khorasan this time of the year. She mentions that the women field workers earn half of what the men make. "It's an Islamic republic," she says, kneeling next to the samovar in her navy sweater, skirt, black stockings, and navy wimple. "The prophet said when a two-year-old boy dies, the killers pay twice the blood money that they would pay for a woman, even if she's a university professor," she says. She looks at me, her dark eyes knowing. "Well, then. This is how it goes."

"When the Koran speaks, it is the word of God, not the prophet," Afzal interjects, sensitive to the implied criticism of his beloved Islam.

Inured by now to what seems to be Afzal's blind spot around issues of religion, I turn back to Mrs. Nobari. "Why don't you change this practice?" I ask.

"I told the men, the women do twice as much work as you do. The pay should be the same."

"And did things change?"

"Of course not." She shrugs. "It's an Islamic republic."

"But you're the landowners," I say, never one to let well enough alone. "It's up to you to make a change."

An uncomfortable silence falls. Mr. Nobari, lounging against the wall as he smokes a cigarette with silent enjoyment, makes some comment about the shortage of agricultural workers. The conversation continues, safely centered on innocuous topics. Mrs. Nobari refills our tea glasses. Then she says to Afzal, "So, Gelareh comes back after so many years. She is much changed, is she?"

I tense, waiting for his answer. I have been listening to variations of this question since I arrived in Iran. My family expected me to return from abroad imbued with the superiority of the West; they expected me to consider myself too good for my family, country, and friends. They expected to agree with me, albeit resentfully.

"Not one bit," Afzal says definitively. "She is the same as she always was."

I feel like a defendant the moment after the jury announces a "not guilty" verdict. I smile down at my tea glass, blinking back sudden tears.

It doesn't matter that he is wrong, that I have changed. Afzal is saying that whatever else I might have become, I am still Iranian.

AFZAL wakes me while the room is still dark. "Get up, get up," he mumbles, half asleep. "We'll be late."

I look at my travel clock. It's two A.M. "Go back to bed," I tell him. "It's not time yet." After I show him the clock, Afzal sleepwalks back to his bedroll across the room and crawls under the quilt with a sigh of relief.

A little past dawn he wakes me again. This time he's fully awake and mischievous. "Why did you wake me up in the middle of the night?" he says. "Don't you have a clock? Get up, get up." He leaves the room when he is sure I am awake. I emerge reluctantly from the warmth of my *rakht-e-khab*— ·the quilt and mattress and pillow unrolled each night at bedtime. I dress in warm layers, grateful for once for the wimple that keeps my head so warm. Metal rings screech when I pull aside the curtain over the doorway, trying to open the wooden door to the corridor without too much clanking and creaking. As soon as I manage to release the vertical latch, the two halves of the door fall open with a bang. I cringe, mutter "Sorry" to whoever's listening, and search for my hiking boots in the communal pile of shoes just outside the door. My frozen fingers, parched from the desert air, fumble with the laces. Shivering, I step into the corridor and out into the walled garden.

As cold as our room seemed, the clear air outside is colder. My breath smokes, my teeth start to chatter. Wrapping my arms about myself, I stand still for a moment, marveling that I inhabit in the flesh a place that has lived so long only in memory. I crane my neck to stare at the navy sky, still studded with countless stars despite the light that blooms gradually in the East. This clear darkness just before light, this mingling of starlight and sunlight, all of it framed by the distinctive silhouette of the tangled trees of my grandfather's garden, is infinitely precious to me. I long to hold on to it, to immemorialize it somehow. But the cold banishes sentiment, and I hurry across the still courtyard to the bathhouse, giving silent thanks that I don't have to venture into the cobwebbed, smelly outhouse we used when I was a child.

The electric light in the new *hammam* seems unbearably harsh, glancing blindingly off the white tiles. A column of black ants streams busily across the floor. I brush my teeth and wash my face in the cold briny water. A shower at this hour is out of the question. Besides, the fields will be dusty.

We rattle off in a borrowed car, Afzal, myself, Ramin, and Ali. The rest of my cousins were not willing to rise so early, though my aunts and Ali's mother kneel silently at their morning prayers, their fingers clicking over worry beads.

The town square is empty of its usual flow of motorcycles, cars and bicycles. We drive through the stillness, emerging soon into wide open fields that glow purple on the horizon. During the saffron harvest, even Gonabad's refuse piles are purple with the scented petals discarded in favor of the red-gold stamens that will be ground to make the spice. Schools open late this time of the year, allowing Gonabad's children to work in the fields, picking the flowers before the sun's heat wilts them.

By the time we reach Mr. Nobari's well, the sun is in the sky and the workers have been picking for a couple of hours. The slanting morning light gilds half of the field while the other half remains in shadow. Afzal and my cousins stand talking with Mr. Nobari, but I want to pick saffron. The farmer, smiling, leads me over to a small group of village women. They cackle delightedly at the idea of my sharing their labors. ("Foreign lady," an aged workman at the construction site on the corner called me when I harangued him for dumping debris in my grandfather's garden during our long absence, his curious, humorous eyes sizing up my clothes and voice and sunglasses.)

The women are squatting next to a row of the flowers, seemingly unhampered by the veils they wear over wimples, sweaters, dresses, and pants. One shy young girl lends me her rusted tin, which originally held a few gallons of lard. A sunburned woman with dry, chapped hands and a mustard yellow sweater shows me how to pick the blossoms so that the stems remain whole, allowing for the longest stamens—an important factor, since saffron is sold by weight.

Kneeling in the damp grass, my shirt and sweater bunching up under my veil, my camera knocking against my chest, my cold fingers sift through the cool silken petals, through grass and dirt. The flowers look just like crocuses. I pick, move crabwise, and pick again, a purple pile growing slowly in the tin can. Caught up in the simple joy of the moment, I forget my self-consciousness. Now and then I pause to watch the morning light advancing along the meadow.

When the sun is high in the sky, we say our farewells. I walk to the car, savoring the peace of the morning. We head back toward town, our destination this time a little cluster of mud houses outside Gonabad. One of the houses belongs to my mother's cousin Haj Abdolkareem Ghassemi. Yesterday, during a courtesy visit to his home, we invited ourselves for breakfast. Haj Abdolkareem's wife, Jahan-Sultan, is waiting for us at the door to her courtyard, standing under a tree as she chats with a neighbor. The tracery of leaves above her head creates patterns of light and shadow that play across her white veil and weathered face. We enter the enclosure, where chickens peck the dirt and tart barberries glow like jewels on their short and prickly trees. At the entrance to the house, Haj Abdolkareem greets us wearing a black wool cap over his gray head, charcoal pants, blue shirt, and navy vest. In the sunny parlor, the white lace curtain has been gathered to the side and secured in a knot. The morning light streams across red-gold bunches of saffron laid out carefully to dry.

The samovar is already steaming in the corner. The square bulk of an Arj oil stove takes up much of one wall. On top, two big kettles of water dispense welcome condensation into the room. Haj Abdolkareem makes a show of sitting by the samovar to dispense tea but yields immediately to his wife when she shoos him away. Their daughter, hiding shyly behind her veil, steps forward quickly to take over her mother's task. As the girl doles out tiny glasses of tea in their chased metal holders, Haj Abdolkareem settles comfortably against a large cushion with one knee bent before him so that he can rest his arm on it, the fingers of that hand thumbing through worry beads. I watch the tea ritual with pleasure, admiring the young woman's ability to keep her veil between her teeth so that she can use both hands without sacrificing modesty. As soon as our glasses are empty, she starts over, rinsing the glasses one by one with hot water flowing from the samovar's spout, then emptying the excess in the metal bowl beneath. She wields the flowered china teapot once again, pouring fresh tea.

Jahan-Sultan bustles back and forth from the kitchen, bringing tray after tray of food. She sets out glasses of steaming cocoa on the vinyl *sofreh*, accompanied by soft-boiled eggs, white country butter, cheese, and *sarshir*, the rich fat skimmed off milk that is a local specialty. She has made the quince and apple jams herself, she tells us. A platter of *kotlet* appears, the meat and potato patties still hot and greasy from the frying pan. There are fresh herbs from the garden and thick rounds of homemade bread. "Have some cocoa, do!" Jahan-Sultan urges me. She repeats the statement for each of the delectable items spread before us. Most of the time, our mouths are too full to answer properly. I watch her rosy face with the permanent frown line between thin, penciled eyebrows, and I feel a twinge of guilt at how much work we have put her to.

When Jahan-Sultan sits at last, she complains of lack of sleep. "He ate what he shouldn't and was up all night, kept me up as well," she says, jerking her head toward Haj Abdol-kareem.

Her husband ignores her, talking instead to Afzal, who is greatly respected here for his university learning. "We had good news last night," Haj Abdolkareem is saying. "The road to Karbala is open again." This holy site has been closed to Iranians for more than twelve years because it is in Iraq.

Afzal tells the old man that I am a writer in America and very much interested in the saffron harvest. Haj Abdolkareem is silent for a moment. Then he says, "If you are preparing a report on the saffron, I have one request. This saffron, when it blooms, is a delicious food. These desert mice eat the bulbs and do a great deal of damage. There's been nothing we have been able to do about it." I respond sympathetically, although I'm smiling at the idea of telling American readers about Go-nabadi mice.

He goes on to tell me about my grandmother, whom I never knew. Homajoon told me once that a jealous acquaintance dubbed her "the Queen of Gonabad." By all accounts, she was a formidable woman. Haj Abdolkareem's cloudy brown eyes fill with tears as he tells me how "the lady" urged his parents to send him to school instead of keeping him in the fields. "If I have bread today it is thanks to your grandmother," the old man tells me. "Otherwise, I would have been illiterate."

After breakfast, our host brings out a new book, *The History and Geography of Gonabad*, and we chuckle over Gona-badi aphorisms. My favorite one goes like this: "If you wish to know the pleasure of sleep, lay your head in the shade and your bum in the sun." Listening to his mellow voice with its rich inflections and the delightful idiosyncrasies of the Gonabadi dialect, I wish, as I have since childhood, that I could talk that way. But I am a city girl and know all too little of the heart of Iran.

THAT night I lie under the comforting weight of my quilt in the darkness, listening to the sounds of life that fill this old house once again. I hear Ramin in the courtyard as he walks to the bathroom, his slippers shuffling across the flagstones. I hear Khaleh Farah's sleepy voice calling out to him: "Make sure you leave a light on in the *hammam*." Two rooms down, an annoyed Ali is telling the younger men, engaged in rowdy horseplay, to settle down.

The last lights go out. The house is dark. I watch the light from the flames in the oil stove flickering across the ceiling, illuminating the room with a warm red glow. Wrapping my quilt more snugly around my body, I feel like a child again, content and secure.

As I drift off to sleep, I can still hear, mingling with the hissing of the flames, the hushed laughter of my cousins Laleh and Soodabeh, sharing secrets into the night.

MY AUNTS do not want me to go to the family's old farm at Kalateh, once the highlight of our visits to Gonabad. The farm was sold several years ago without my knowledge. I reproached Homajoon bitterly when I found out. She did not defend herself, instead looking wistful and sad. Kalateh cannot possibly be the same, yet I need to see it with my own eyes.

It is not until we get there, asking directions two or three times, swallowing dust as our little borrowed Gian cuts across fields, that I realize my folly. My mind said all would be changed. But my heart believed, childlike, that it would still be there, waiting—the rows of Russian olive trees rippling silver in the wind, the deep pool with its quicksilver fish, the stream that ran under a mud wall and into the pond. In that pond, my sister and I were set afloat by my uncles, happy naked babies cradled in automobile tires.

All of these things I somehow expect to see. So when my eyes take in the ragged children, the carcass of a sheep rotting in the noonday sun next to a squalid hut, the mangy dogs, the pile of sand where the pond used to be—they quarry it here—the shock feels like a physical blow. I want to retch. I walk very fast, heading into the middle of a cotton field, as if the green plants around me can wipe away the sense of witnessing an obscenity. My cousin Ali follows me, his face somber. I keep my back to him. The sun beating down on my black-covered head feels too hot, too bright.

"I told my aunts not to sell," Ali says morosely. "I asked them to let me get a permit for a well, to try to farm the land. But they said no."

I nod silently. I find tissues in the pocket of my *roupoush*, a cotton overcoat like the ones schoolgirls and government workers wear.

"Let's go," I say abruptly, and stride to the car.

CONVERSATION during a visit from relatives:

Mr. Zabihi: "In your view, what will come of this matter with Iraq and Kuwait?"

Afzal: "I believe the end result will be that Amrika and the Western nations will gain permanent control of Saudi Arabia and Kuwait so that they can have a free flow of oil."

WE WALK by the corner fruit and vegetable store on our way out. Business is brisk. Afzal nods to the owner, shepherds us into the bus, and tells the driver where to go. First stop: the café, to return the empty bottles of soda we've consumed the past few days. Second: the drugstore, where Afzal, pronounc-

ing himself to be a doctor (which he is, of French literature),
picks up some antibiotics for his cold. We drive through town,
past the movie theater where *Thief of Dolls* is the featured at-
traction, and hit the open highway. I gaze out the window at
the dry landscape, gilded in the morning sun. The mountains
are purple in the distance.

When we arrive, Mr. Nobari is standing by the pool, watching the light play on the water. He is smoking one of his unfil-
tered Tir cigarettes. The farmer's wool hat is set loosely on the
back of his head, rising into a peak. His only concession to the
November chill is a gray scarf and a sweater under his suit
jacket. As soon as greetings have been exchanged, we strike
out across the fields, Afzal walking with Mr. Nobari.

We walk for a long time, past short, stubby pistachio trees
with their scaly leaves, past rows of thorny barberry bushes.
The berries seems luminous, lit translucently by the sun shining through red fruit and a fine sheen of dust. In the distance I
can see patches of purple where a few fields of saffron still wait
to be picked. Here and there a chicken feather clings to a bush,
fluttering in the breeze. Bits of blackened paper and feathery
ash drift from the brief, intense fires the field hands light to
warm their hands and feet. The blazes seem transparent in
the sunlight.

Past the fields, the ground is bare but for the bone-white
thorn bushes that folks collect at winter's end, burning them
in the bonfires that celebrate the end of the old year. Each time
my boots meet the ground, I am aware of the planet beneath
my feet, revealed here in its most elemental form. Elsewhere
there are cities and forests and oceans, ships and stock exchanges and shopping malls. Elsewhere there are scientists
and politicians, rock stars, busy parents dropping off their children at preschool.

But here in Gonabad, there is only the sun and the wind and
an infinity of land and sky.

II · Homecoming: America

Silver Spring, Maryland
December 1, 1990

I T IS six A.M. I am downstairs in the basement of our house, nursing a mug of cooling tea and trying to avoid looking at the naked ductwork above my head. Neil and I have never figured out what to do about the exposed pipes that are suspended almost a foot below the basement's low ceiling. We moved into this house two years ago, a few months after leaving Miami for Silver Spring. Just married, we were thrilled to have a home of our own.

I lie on the green couch in front of the silent television set, busying my mind with possible solutions to the familiar dilemma of the exposed pipes. The distraction helps me to reconnect with my life here in America, allows me to avoid what I am feeling. I have been alternating between insomnia and torpor ever since I returned from Iran two days ago. An eight-and-a-half-hour time change and twenty-six hours in transit are only part of the reason.

I am unraveling. I have come back to my house, my job, and my husband, but my life seems bleak to me. I ache for the blue sky over Gonabad. I think of my family gathered around the *sofreh* and my heart contracts with longing. I miss the talk, the squabbling, the laughter, the houses that were never empty.

I pull the pink flowered quilt I begged from Khaleh Mina closer around me and burrow deeper into the couch. The cool slippery surface and the bright flowers blooming across the fabric are marginally comforting.

When I was in Iran, I couldn't stand that the houses were never empty. Now I suffer from a surfeit of emptiness. A great fear rises in my gorge. What am I doing here in this country with its silent neighborhoods and disconnected families? What am I doing married to a man who doesn't speak my language?

I prepared myself for culture shock when I went to Iran after so many years in America. Instead, the culture that now seems alien is the one it took me so long to make my own. It all comes crashing down around me, the persona I assembled with such difficulty in those first years after moving to America.

Some days later, back at work, I pull out my press pass to enter the Maryland capitol in Annapolis, where I am covering the governor's press conference. As I prepare to restore the card to my wallet, I look at the woman smiling brightly beneath plastic and wonder how I know her.

She is a false self constructed to hide the fractured chaos beneath. She is a casualty of my trip to Iran.

New York

How was your trip?" asks my oldest, my first, friend here in America.

I answer at length, rambling. I am sitting across the table

from my friend and her husband, Neil at my side. We're in the Russian Tea Room. Muted light gleams on my friend's jewelry, on the antique gold color of her hair, on the soft cream-colored sweater she wears. The people at the other tables are similarly poised and well dressed.

I want to savor the elegance of this room. Instead, I am filled with a sense of unbelonging. My friends, my husband, seem alien to me, as if fashioned from different clay. I watch myself talking, watch them responding, sip my drink, and feel a wave of hopelessness. Nothing I say can describe for them what my trip was like. America long ago ceased to be impenetrable to me. But my essence seems impenetrable to even my closest friends here in America. I am afraid that my need to be known by those I love is destined to be frustrated, whether I am with my Iranian family of origin or the family I started when I married. Even Neil can only guess at a reality so far beyond his grasp.

Outside, we step into a frigid winter night. I pull up the collar of my coat. It is the black Persian lamb that I bought in Mashad, and its softness comforts me. I trail behind the others, walking with my chin tucked into my coat.

Passing a glass skyscraper, I instinctively seek my own reflection. What I see is a solitary, distorted shape trapped in glass.

FOR months I keep the dust of Iran in my shoes, and it makes me miserable.

Gradually I let go. I channel my anguish into trying to infuse some Iranianness into days that feel almost totally American. I buy Iranian tapes. I start praying again, for a time. I renew my attempts to teach Neil Farsi. It is a pattern that will become familiar in the course of subsequent trips to Iran.

One day I wake up and there is joy to life again.

I have stopped fighting forgetfulness. It seeps into my life, insulating me from the reality of an unbridgeable chasm.

I have reconstructed my facade.

Cumberland, Maryland
1990

CONVERSATION with a police secretary I've met while covering a jail break, after we've finished debating the merits of our husbands and moved on to the trouble in the Mideast:

"You know, it says in the Bible those people over there are descended from jackals," she says, blue eyes wide and earnest.

I look at her as if I'm seeing her for the first time.

"Actually, I'm from over there," I say. "And we're not descended from jackals."

She stares at me, speechless.

Neither of us has much to say to each other after that.

Baltimore
1991

CONVERSATION with a colleague at the *Baltimore Sun:* "You're Iranian?" he asks, surprised. I nod.

There is a long pause. He looks at the TV screen above the City Desk, mute since the evening news is not yet on. Then he turns back to me. "I have nothing against the Iranian people."

I want to say: Thank you for granting me benediction.

But this is someone I work with.

I smile stiffly and walk back to my desk.

CONVERSATION with a colleague's husband at an office party:

"I had a roommate once who was Iranian," he says with a smile. "He was really nice."

He sounds surprised.

CONVERSATION with a friend after we've seen the movie *Not Without My Daughter*.

"I can't believe that movie," I say, seething. It was filmed in dark colors and depicted every Iranian as uncouth and angry except for one man who had gone to school in the West. The movie implied that Iranian men routinely beat their wives.

My friend did not notice the stereotypes.

"Isn't that the way it is over there?" he says.

III · Childhood

Sunday, 15 Khordad, Imperial Year 2536, Lunar Year 1953 (June 5, 1974)

My Life story: I am an Iranian girl living in Teheran the capital of Iran. Age: Out of 12. Class: second of guidance school. School: Iran-Suisse at the moment. I love this school because it has become familiar to me and also I love the kids here. I also like the ways, good or bad. Bye, I don't feel like writing anymore . . .

T HE summer I was twelve, my biggest problem was boredom—how to make one birthday party, two swim dates, a movie, and an outing to the skating rink at the Ice Palace last me through the long weeks before school started again. I worried about boys and their lack of attendance at birthday parties. Climbing into my bathing suit for the first time since the previous summer, I resolved in my journal to eat less ice cream and chocolate. I decided to write my life story. I spent too many hours in bed. I complained for days when Homajoon told me that Khaleh Mina was to visit and that she and the boys would be staying in my room. "They'll ruin all my things!" I yelled. "Don't be selfish!" my mother remonstrated. But I was. My own concerns swaddled me like a baby, shutting out the larger world.

I wrote in my journal in English. In that summer of 1974, we had been back from the United States for a little over two years. At school, classmates had stopped mocking my "Amri-kayi" accent. I was happy for the first time since 1970.

It was in 1970 that both my parents received letters of admission to the University of North Carolina at Chapel Hill, Baba in the School of Public Health, Homajoon in the School of Library Science. For my parents, it was the realization of a dream. With great excitement they took out a loan, packed up the house, and moved us to North Carolina for two years.

Our pictures from that period show my family squinting against an unfamiliar sun. The backdrops are varied, but the expressions are the same: strained and sad. There is the picture of Homajoon under the dogwood tree in the front yard on my eighth birthday, when I was conspicuously overdressed in blue satin. My mother looks troubled and weary. There is the picture from Duke Gardens: pink-blossoming trees and my sister Afsaneh and I posed side by side on a low branch, staring glumly into the distance. There is a snapshot of my father pushing us on the swing set in the overgrown back yard of the house we rented that first year. Afsaneh and I were outraged at the absence of walls—"What do you mean, anybody can walk across our lawn?" Certainly, walls would have kept out the anonymous person—probably the girl next door—who scrawled "I hate you" in the gravel of our driveway.

There is the family photo in front of the Washington Monument, the four of us braced against the bluster of a chilly autumn day.

The few smiles are forced, usually in the presence of others, as in the photo of Homajoon and a classmate standing in front of the library science building. The only exception was when we joined a gathering of the welcoming crowd of Iranians who lived in Chapel Hill and its environs. They were strange to us because they moved comfortably in a world we found alien; because they seemed unconscious, even when Afsaneh and I stifled giggles, of the English words that littered their Farsi conversation. But they were familiar, too: their eyes and skin and hair, their history, their words. They were a bridge between America and Iran.

I went to America knowing less than a handful of words in English. Afsaneh, two and a half years my senior, knew slightly more. It is no wonder, then, that school was a misery. I remember Baba's taking me to the school cafeteria for the first time: his hand holding mine as we confronted the noise, the strange faces turned our way, the fluorescence, the white walls. I was both comforted and distressed by my father's presence. The other children would see in a glance that my *baba* was different. His foreignness and vulnerability were visible in his dark skin (I did not consider it dark until we moved to America), in the uncertainty of his carriage, in his sweater and pants that were indefinably different from what Americans wore. I pulled my hand out of his, muttering in Farsi that I was fine. But Baba stood protectively over me while I drank milk through a straw placed in a little red carton. The milk was bland and tasted like cardboard; it coated my tongue with a chalky film. I have hated the taste ever since.

By the second year, my sister and I spoke fluent English. My family moved into an apartment in university housing. It had dark brown couches in fake leather, a bunk bed with prison-stripe mattresses for my sister and me, and linoleum floors. Here, there were children who actually deigned to play with us. Here, there were good days as well as the bad ones. After one particularly bad day, I sat on the steps of our apartment building and cried, telling Afsaneh how much I wanted to go home to Iran. She responded brusquely, turning her back on my tears, as if my vulnerability were contagious. I did not blame her. After all, I said nothing the day the Afghan boy down the street stumbled from the school bus, crying, even after the sniggering blonde girl next to me mimicked his dark-eyed mother when she ran after the bus, calling angrily, "Why you hit my good boy?"

It was bliss to come home to Tehran, to eyes filled with tears of gladness, arms reaching to hold me, forgotten toys and books miraculously disgorged from the boxes we had left behind. My parents had earned their master's degrees; Baba's in public health administration, Homajoon's in library science. This was a good thing, since both had to go to work immediately to pay off our accumulated debts. All in all, it had been a successful, if painful, venture.

My sister and I had to take tests to determine our placement in Iranian schools, but we were prepared for this. We drove home from the United States after crossing the ocean on a liner that carried our brand-new yellow Ford Mustang, and our schoolbooks accompanied us on the ship and in the car. We drove through Turkey, and as we waited at the border with Iran, I vividly remember Baba's admonishing me to study my math. I did well enough to enter fifth grade, as my age dictated. Homajoon and Baba decided to send both of us to Iran-Suisse Academy, the moderately tony private school my cousins attended.

There I discovered how greatly my fortunes had changed. Overnight I went from being an inferior, shunned being to that most envied of creatures in Iran, a girl just back from America. A lot of the teasing about my Amrikayi accent—although I did tend to slur my Farsi words that first year home—stemmed from envy. My classmates didn't know how grateful I was to be back in a place where I could belong. In those days it was Iran, not America, that held luster in my eyes.

With my cousin Reza in the same class, I adjusted quickly. I loved school, the mandatory uniforms, the asphalt playground where we played dodgeball, the half-days on Thursday—the beginning of the Iranian weekend —that invariably ended in unsanctioned water fights. The schoolyard on Kakh Street filled with shrieks and laughter, and clusters of children in drenched gray and white uniforms huddled at the metal gate as the grownups strolled up to fetch their charges. Adults would bend and speak one word in the ear of the doorman, a short, slender man in a worn suit and sweater whose eyes were always scrunched against the afternoon sun. He would lift his red megaphone to his lips and call out the name ("*ASA-YESHHHH!*"), nodding us through the gate and into the weekend. My cousins and my sister and I would greet Mr. Khandani, the cheery driver assigned to Baba as part of his perks as a senior bureaucrat at the Ministry of Health. As soon as Mr. Khandani unlocked the doors of the blue Jeep station wagon, we'd clamber in, shivering, and focus our energies on persuading him to stop at the corner store for treats. If he gave in, we would buy butter toffees, plastic packages of tamarind paste, bags of nuts and seeds, or the handmade fruit rolls called *lavashak*. In the springtime we bought greengages and green almonds from the carts of traveling vendors, the tart green fruit gleaming and crowned with salt in newspaper twisted into a cone. Our teachers and parents warned us that the fruit was likely to be dirty, washed in ditch water (they said). But it was crisp and delicious and we didn't care.

I loved school because I was a social being, because I thrived on rules and regulations. I loved it because I did well in class and because I made friends. But I loved it more than anything because it restored the self-esteem annihilated in two years in America. I was home again and I was in my element. In that summer of 1974, more than at any other time in my life, I belonged.

As a child, I was fascinated with the English language. It seemed to me inconceivable that anyone could speak it. English was exotic, evoking unimaginable delights in a faraway land. I remember running along a Caspian beach once when I was about seven, pretending that I spoke it fluently. I summoned my entire vocabulary, learned in first-grade English classes, as I ran, my legs pumping as if they could muster the fluency my tongue lacked. "Stop!" I cried. "Go!" "Surprise!"

After our sojourn abroad, the English language became mine. It did not happen overnight. That first year in Chapel Hill, my sister and I moved in a fog of incomprehension. The people around us shared codes that we could not break. My family spent most of one afternoon around our Formica dining table, trying in vain to puzzle out the meaning of the word "y'all." (It was years later, on our return to Chapel Hill, that we realized it was a contraction of "you all.") I remember sitting with Afsaneh in front of the TV screen, watching an episode of *Hee Haw* with eager perplexity. After Iran, where the highlight of the television week was the Friday afternoon movie, American television was a feast we were hungry for. We watched a lot of bad television, and we made innumerable mistakes when we spoke English. I can still remember my classmates at Estes Hills Elementary tittering when I read the word "bird," pronouncing it "beard." They wondered, out loud, where I'd come from that I was so ignorant of this most basic fact of their lives, that "ir" was pronounced "er."

But little by little the language yielded its secrets to us. By the time we returned to Tehran, English was the language in which my sister and I communicated best. It was the language of our private exchanges, our furious fights and games and bargains ("If you give me the rest of your Three Musketeers bar, I'll scratch your back tonight . . .").

From the day we returned home, going back to America was on our horizon. After all, you were not truly upper middle class in Iran unless you sent your children abroad to study. Despite my joy in being back, despite the misery of my experience there, I dreamed of America. I was nostalgic for the forests, for ice cream sandwiches, for Levi's—for the places and the opportunities rather than the people. As first my cousins and then several friends were dispatched to schools in England, Switzerland, and America, I begged to go abroad. My parents shook their heads, making no promises. I did not know that they fully intended to send us to college in the United States. They kept their plans to themselves, for they faced enormous hurdles, both financial and personal. They were making the hardest choice of their lives: to send us away as so many Iranian families did, trusting us to negotiate the perils of an alien culture, or to give up their jobs, home, and families to accompany us.

I was oblivious of these concerns. This is what strikes me most, looking through my journals from that time with the puzzled, detached fascination of someone examining moon rocks. In the way of all children, I lived wholly in the present. I could not imagine other ways of being. College, America, packing up and leaving Iran, were all cardboard concepts with little meaning.

My life, my culture, fit me like my skin. It was as impossible then for me to comprehend a day when I would be a stranger to myself as it is now, looking back over the years, to comprehend my own innocence.

THE topography of my life in those days was simple. Six days a week, my cousins and sister and I would pile into the blue station wagon to go to school. After school the empty hours stretched interminably until Homajoon and Baba came home at night, tired and frazzled from the traffic, the latest family conflict, office politics, and other adult concerns. Their bedroom light would go on, a warm glow in the dark and silent house. Afsaneh and I gravitated toward that light, to the room where Homajoon undressed behind the mahogany door of the armoire while Baba, whistling softly, made a slow transition from suit and bow tie to the pajamas he wore around the house. He would sit on the edge of the bed and methodically polish his shoes before putting them away, alternating between the smooth leather and his daughters' shining hair, the two of us twining around him like cats. Their bedroom wall was painted a pale yellow. I sat there in total contentment, warmed by the light, the yellow walls, the presence of Homajoon and Baba.

Over their bed, a wide window opened into the greenhouse where potted plants were stored in winter. The crowded greenery behind panes of glass held a special allure for me. I associated it with Friday mornings when, the work week ended, my parents would sleep late and my sister and I would crawl into their bed. With eyes closed and morning breath and a rusty voice, Baba would tell us the story of the mouse and the lion. It is a story that is lost to all of us now, though I still remember my delight at the ingenious rope pulley the two friends rigged, somehow saving the day. A rope pulley gleaming whitely in the green jungle haze, just as that one detail of a forgotten story gleams in the murk of my memory.

In winter, when snow fell, I would step into the greenhouse to breathe in the green summer smell. Its warm moisture was good for thawing frozen fingers and toes. On mornings after a night of snow, our servant Naneh would summon a *paroo-zan*, one of the men who go door to door with their wooden paddles, offering to sweep roofs and driveways. From the flat roof he swept so much snow that the two levels of our front yard—the porch sitting three steps above the gardens—became one. My cousins came over to play, and Afsaneh and Reza and Mehra and I took turns leaping into that pile of snow, celebrating with loud shrieks that school was canceled for the day.

Our house was built on a steep hill. From the moment the car pulled through the metal gate and we stepped out, we were climbing: first the sloping driveway, then the twenty-three steps to the yard and more steps leading from the tiered garden to the porch and into the house itself. An encircling wall separated our domain from the alley beyond. Iranian houses are walled for privacy. This way, even the most devout women can go about their chores with their heads uncovered.

In our house, this was not an issue. My mother and my sister and I never wore scarves, let alone veils, except in religious settings and in the small provincial towns where people expected it of us. Naneh, the only other woman in the house, never bared her head. She had served my family ever since I could remember. She would have looked undressed without her close fitting wimple, her vest decorated with pierced coins on safety pins, her loose dress worn over cotton trousers. Naneh's eyes were rheumy, her shoulders perpetually bent, and her clothes imbued with the warm smell of her body, sweat and dust and an occasional bitter tang of opium. Homajoon gave her a stick each Norooz—the government ban on the drug, after all, excluded aged addicts like Naneh and my grandfather. The opium was dark and smooth, like a giant, bitter-smelling Tootsie Roll.

Naneh smoked her opium in her little room in the back of the house that opened off the tiny back yard. The *hayat khalvat* or the "private yard" was a dingy place where we kept the giant oil drum that held our winter fuel. This was replenished at regular intervals by the *nafti*, the oil man who labored up the steps with sweat pouring off his neck and the drum balanced on one knotted shoulder. A metal stairway led from the yard to the asphalt roof, a place I loved. On the way up, the steps sounded hollow beneath my feet. Gravel crunched underfoot on the tarred concrete when I stepped on the roof, trading the close gloom of the back yard for a vista.

On one side, I could see the patchwork of neighbors' roofs and backyards climbing up toward the mountains. The mountains were the silent sentinels of my childhood, dun gray in the summer and snowcapped in winter. They gave us perspective, their timeless majesty an ever-present contrast to our little lives.

On the other side of the roof, our front garden was a green jewel set in the dry hillside. In the distance, the ugly-beautiful city of my birth sprawled beneath a gasoline haze, a hodgepodge of gray and brown and beige relieved by occasional splashes of green.

The daily routine of our lives was broken by frequent parties, when the house was filled with the sounds of conversation and laughter. These events usually involved Afsaneh's and my dusting Homajoon's sizable collection of African animals and every leaf of every plant in the house, so we did not look forward to them. But I loved listening to my parents' laugh, for it happened too rarely.

In warm weather, our guests would assemble on the porch, where pots of jasmine scented the twilight and Homajoon served cold concoctions of crushed melon and ice or tall, chill glasses of syrups—sour cherry, lemon, mint, and quince. I liked to listen to the sound of teaspoons clinking against glass as our guests stirred their drinks, clouds of apricot and magenta syrup diffusing through the cold water, the tiny crushed seeds added as digestive aids swirling madly. Parties were held in the front garden, the only part of our house that was truly lovely. I dreamed about that garden for years after we left: the green grass, the beds of pansies, the cherry trees and the weeping willows rustling in the breeze. I loved to comb my fingers through the willow leaves, feeling their smooth texture. The trees were as important to my world as my friends, even though I grumbled every time I had to water them with the garden hose, lingering on the lawn as the sun set and the clear water pooled at the bases of each woody trunk and stray grass stems settled between my bare wet toes. In springtime, when the white cherry blossoms mingled ethereally with the soft pink blooms of Japanese quince, I would stand for long moments on the way to school, drinking in the sight. Toward summertime, when fruit gleamed like a promise among the green leaves of the cherry trees, I would come home from school, grab the stepladder from the storeroom, drag it outside, and set it against the tree of my choice. There I would sit, in my gray and white uniform, my fingers questing greedily through the dusty leaves, my hands and mouth sticky with the sweet red fruit.

It tasted of dust. It tasted of summer. It tasted of joy.

AFTER we moved to the United States, my mother and sister and I spent years searching unsuccessfully for jasmine like the plants that bloomed on our porch in Iran, white blossoms with a dizzying fragrance. But as children, Afsaneh and I hated our daily chore: to pick the flowers while they were still fresh, before the morning sun reached its zenith. In the days when my grandmother, Baba's mother, was alive and living with us, she liked to set a bowl of the star-shaped flowers nearby while she prayed. When the bending and straightening of the *namaz* was done, she would sit kneeling for long moments, wrapped in clean white cotton and the scent of jasmine, her fingers clicking through her worry beads and her dry lips murmuring: "God is Great."

In the summer, we slept on the porch, our bedrolls spread next to one another, a mosquito coil sending fumes into the night air. On the nights when someone was willing to carry the heavy bedrolls up the metal stairs, we slept on the roof. I remember climbing up those steps in my pajamas, my teeth freshly brushed, a pillow held to my chest, a glass of water balanced carefully in one hand. Each step carried me deeper into the night. On one side of the roof, the dark mass of the mountains was pierced by a mysterious scattering of lights—army camps, my uncle Abbas told me once. On the other, the city stretched into the distance like a jeweled carpet.

When I lay down on the cool sheets, the weight of my quilt anchored me to earth and I could let myself be swallowed up in the arcing universe above. One sleepless night I watched three meteors flare and die. "You should see the sky from the heart of the desert, far from city lights," my father would say as we counted stars. (If there were too many to count, Baba would say the stars were holding a wedding.) Watching the nostalgia on his face, my heart contracted with wanderlust. I longed to travel all the roads and byways he had traveled, to see what he had seen—for when we were young, Baba was always traveling.

When we slept on the porch, the magnitude of the sky was reduced to a human scale by the comforting silhouette of house and garden. I could hear the wind rustle in the willows all night as my family slept around me. Next to Baba's mattress was a bowl of water filled with ice. "There's nothing like drinking iced water from a bowl," he liked to say, lifting the vessel to his lips with both hands and drinking deep. Growing up on the periphery of Iran's arid core, my parents had a deep appreciation of water. The tinkle of ice and Baba's patent enjoyment made Afsaneh and me immediately dissatisfied with our glasses of water. "It's even better if it's an earthenware bowl," Baba said. "It holds the cold better."

By morning, the ice in Baba's bowl had melted. The quilts that felt comforting in the chill of the night became stifling, and the hot sun and buzzing flies drove us all indoors, yawning and bleary-eyed. Once inside, my sister and I, free of responsibilities, continued to sleep as long as we wanted in the guest room, which was occupied over the course of our childhood by a succession of relatives and friends.

Toward the end of his life, the room belonged to my mother's father, who was frail now, his cheeks sunken. Aghajoon's silence and the bitter smell of the opium brazier kept me away except at dinnertime, when the women—my mother and Bibi, Aghajoon's young wife—would bring him skewers of grilled meat to tempt his waning appetite. I could not understand why he did not gobble up this special fare as I would have, given half a chance. Instead, he sat in his brown pajamas, hands shaking, staring into the distance. He had been ill for a long time, and he was in pain. Khaleh Farah and Khaleh Mina visited from Mashad and sat in the bedroom where my mother knelt on the middle of her prayer rug, just through with her afternoon *namaz*. Homajoon's pretty hands worked nervously on her worry beads as they talked, Khaleh Farah's shoulders were hunched; Khaleh Mina held her veil over her face. I knew she was weeping.

My mother cried so much at my grandfather's funeral that she could barely stand. Her eyes were red and almost closed with puffiness. My own eyes ached in sympathy. Aghajoon was buried under the courtyard of the Mashad shrine. When we visited his grave, my mother would count the tiles until she found the exact spot, then stand there in the middle of the courtyard as she murmured the prayer for the dead, looking lost.

FROM the blue railings at the end of our garden, I could see the alley where boys with close-shaven heads played soccer in their undershirts and baggy pajama bottoms, dirty feet flapping in their slippers, the ball a plastic husk with faded stripes. The alley joined the gravel road that led to the corner supermarket, and from there to the paved thoroughfares of Shemiran. It was from this direction that, hanging over the railing during Muharram, a Shi'ite month of mourning, I heard the sound of chanting. A column of men appeared, walking in a cloud of dust that clung to their black garments. With their hands, they beat their bared chests. Some beat themselves on the back with lengths of chain swung rhythmically. They chanted the name of Hossein, grandson of the prophet Mohammad, who was murdered with his followers in the Arabian desert of Karbala on the tenth of Muharram.

Rituals observing the betrayal and martyrdom of Imam Hossein are the staple of Muharram. Even so, the sound of marching feet and lamenting voices filled me with dread. I wondered if the chains were real and if they hurt. Homajoon, who was home that day, came up quickly and motioned me away from the railing. Her eyebrows were drawn into a frown, her eyes snapped a warning. "Go inside, hurry," she said. "You're wearing red. They might be offended."

I ran to obey her, my sense of guilt automatic. When I dressed that morning, it had never occurred to me that it was Muharram and that subdued colors were the order of the day. I was afraid because Homajoon was afraid. What would have happened if they had seen me? Would their passions, already inflamed, turn into violence?

As I walked up the steps into the house, guilt turned into resentment. Why should something so trivial as the color of my shirt matter? I hated the rigidity of my religion, its messages of shame and blame. Anytime Afsaneh or I questioned Islamic teachings ("What's so terrible about eating pork?"), the women of the family bit their lips and rolled their eyes. If we said something especially heinous, they would strike their thigh in horror and bite the webbed flesh between thumb and forefinger, first with their palm down, then with it facing upward—the ritual gesture of repentance. "Astaghfor-allah!" they exclaimed. "I seek God's forgiveness." I did not know then what the Arabic phrase meant. I did not need to. The message of shocked reproof was clear.

I loved the aspects of my religion that celebrated life. Ramadan, for example, was a time when friends and family, laughing and talking in their black clothes and veils, gathered at sundown to break their fasts with a feast. I was awed and inspired by the concept of fasting and by the faithful way it was carried out all around me. I loved the special foods: the crisp, syrupy saffron pastries made only at this time of year, the dates stuffed with walnuts and sprinkled with coconut, the demitasse cups of Turkish coffee, grainy and sweet, flavored with cocoa and rose water, the flat plates of *halva*, a velvety brown concoction of sugar and flour and saffron gleaming with a sheen of oil—rich foods all, intended to fortify the body for fasting and weeping.

But I hated the gloom and zealotry. My sister and I were endlessly scrutinized and chastised. Did we pray? our religious relatives wanted to know, clucking in disapproval when we stammered, "Sometimes." The veneer of our Western life would crumble at such moments, revealing the religious roots that bound us all. During Muharram, even secular households would hold *rowzehs*, gatherings where the Koran and stories of martyrdom were chanted by mullahs in turbans and flowing brown robes. Their audiences were separated by sex: men in one room with the mullah, women in another close by so they could hear the chanting.

Most of Homajoon's *rowzehs* were exclusively female affairs. I remember our house perfumed with the smell of rose water and coffee, the guest parlor filled with the light voices of women gossiping, Homajoon and her helpers hurrying to and fro bearing laden trays. Then the loose third step in the foyer clunked beneath the heavy footsteps of a man, and a deep voice murmured "Ya'allah" to announce his presence. My mother's guests grabbed their veils as the mullah entered with his slow, ponderous tread. Homajoon, murmuring a greeting, her head bowed deferentially and covered by her white *chador*, showed him to a chair in a place of honor. His eyes avoided the females gathered around him, even the children, guarding against temptation and preserving his holy aura. I felt shamed, as if being a woman were a sin.

The mullah arranged his robes, cleared his throat, and bent his head for a moment. Suddenly, his deep voice lifted in a piercing lament, storytelling mingled with Koranic verse. The women's heads drooped. They pulled their veils closer, hiding their faces. After the appropriate interval of time, shoulders began to shake and the sounds of weeping rose—softly at first and then, in step with the orator's crescendo, more loudly. The women sobbed and wailed in a paroxysm of orchestrated grief. Even as a child, I did not believe they cried for the martyrs of Islam. Imam Hossein's story was a parable of the human condition, a catalyst for their own sadness. They cried over their own losses and tribulations; they cried because it was expected of them and they cried for the same reason some people run—for release. An American friend, visiting once during a *rowzeh*, called the experience "great therapy."

Afsaneh and I were too young to view it with such detachment. As soon as the crying and chanting began, we would escape into the garden. I ran as far away from the house as I could, covering my ears with my hands, fighting a nameless despair that seemed to flow darkly from the guest parlor.

When the crying ceased, I felt overwhelming relief. My sister and I edged back into the parlor, where the red-eyed women wilted in their corners. They seemed subdued but peaceful. Somberly at first, they helped themselves to the passing trays of coffee and sweets. The mullah sat for a while, eating and drinking, then withdrew to the foyer, where he was discreetly paid. As soon as he left, the mood lightened. Gossip and laughter dispelled the gloom. Afsaneh and I lolled against our mother's knee, at ease again.

MY SISTER and I were not allowed to play in the alley. Sheltered by our anxious parents, we were restricted to the walled confines of the house. Our playmates were Reza and Mehra, our cousins. The four of us would have been inseparable except that we lived in separate families. In the house, we played hide-and-seek and cowboys-and-Indians, pointing our fingers for guns. Outside we played soccer and dodgeball.

In the center of the lawn, there was an oval depression where one of the many sewage wells for the house had been dug. Since Tehran had no sewage treatment system, we had to dig a new one every few years. We were warned never to play in that green hollow in case it caved in. We responded by running through it very quickly, our hearts beating just a little bit faster until we were safely across.

Our fear was heightened the day we came home from school to find a crowd gathered in the garage. Caught up in the sensed drama of the moment, we barely noticed the noxious smell that hung over the group. The adult world seemed united in some event that we children could not fathom, troubled by emotions that left us untouched. On a stretcher lay a man's form, covered with a dirty white cloth. Baba's face—I remember wondering what he was doing home from work in the middle of the day—looked grim. He stared straight ahead as the foreman of the well-digging crew talked volubly in his ear.

The crew had arrived that morning to dig the newest sewage well, this time in the garage. The trickiest part of their task was connecting the new well to the existing network. "We told him to come up," the foreman said to Baba, gesturing to the still form on the stretcher. "He said he was going to dig just a little farther."

"God rest his soul," someone muttered.

I watched the two men standing side by side, the foreman with his country dialect and rumpled clothes and the foreign-educated doctor with his smooth face, suit, and bow tie. The foreman's eyes were bright coals in a face that was as dark and leathery as Naneh's. Baba's eyes are a light sherry brown. This characteristic often leads people to defer to him, eager to bequeath to him that special status reserved for Westerners or those who look like them.

Baba received deference not just because of his light eyes, of course. He had social stature as well. First of all, he was a doctor—the most prestigious profession in Iran. Second, as managing director in the Shah's Ministry of Health, he held a position of power. The people who entered Baba's office often clasped their hands subserviently in front, bowing repeatedly. Even if they were his social equals, they asked after his health more fervently than normal. On the rare occasions when my sister and I visited his office, with its acre-long conference table and potted plants, we were the beneficiaries of his status, petted and complimented by secretaries and lesser bureaucrats. A servant in an open-necked white shirt immediately went off to bring tea and biscuits, and Afsaneh and I stared in awe at Baba, barely recognizing our doting father at the center of all this power and responsibility.

Homajoon also occupied a position of power and responsibility, if on a smaller scale. As head of the medical library in the health ministry, her fiefdom was confined to a handful of young women who wore too-short mini-skirts and too much makeup. They had carefully coiffed dark hair and seemed more interested in finding husbands than in their work, much to my mother's frustration. She did her best to nudge them toward a sense of professionalism, with mixed results.

When Homajoon sat at her desk, a thin, weather-beaten man named Mr. Khandan brought her tea and biscuits and his occasional tales of woe. Softhearted and sincere, my mother always tried to help him. She must have succeeded, because in her presence Mr. Khandan seemed to overflow with gratitude. Despite his limited means, he tried to reciprocate through the eagerness with which he served her and the turquoise plastic comb that he once bought for her.

My sister and I grew up taking for granted our relatively elevated place in Iran's stratified society. But in my parents' household, it was clear that status entailed responsibility. Acquaintances and friends who were down on their luck always turned to my parents for help. The lower-class ones hunkered down in the kitchen, the women weeping into a corner of their veils as they related their misfortunes. The middle-class ones were received in the family room. My parents doled out tea, cash, medicine, and job references. My sister and I were expected to stop by long enough to say hello. The men bowed to us, but the women would reach workworn hands to our heads, pulling us down for tearful embraces. They showed their gratitude to Homajoon and Baba by calling down blessings upon their daughters. It was the way of Iran: prayers and subservience in exchange for patronage. None of the drivers, washerwomen, maids, and laborers who came to the kitchen would ever have dreamed of sitting down at the table with us. And, for all her kindness, Homajoon would never have asked them to. It just wasn't done. The Western egalitarianism that I read about in my novels seemed to be one of the few imports that had no place in our way of life.

When I look back on those years, it is with piercing nostal-

gia. We lived the life we pleased, and we lived in Iran. It was
not one or the other. We may have attracted leers and averted
gazes in our mini-skirts, but no one kept us from wearing
them. Traditional Iranians avoided places like Cabaret Miami, where diners carried the smell of alcohol on their breaths
and the pop star Gougoush sang in spangled off-the-shoulder
dresses, but no one closed these places down. Men and women
mingled freely at pool parties and weekend retreats to lush
gardens. Each summer we visited the Caspian shore, where
women in bikinis were a jarring and titillating sight to the
sunburned countryfolk who spent their life growing tea in the
hills and rice in the paddies. We skied at Dizin. We went skating at Ice Palace, where young people crowded up to the
counters for burgers and fries. We savored Pêche Melba at the
poolside restaurant at Hotel Vanak.

And each vacation we visited Mashad and Gonabad and rev-
eled in the joys of family life. Each Muharram we held our *rowzehs*. Each day, we unfolded our prayer rugs when the call to
prayer summoned.

It is easy to feel, looking back, that we had it all—the pleasures of the West and the rootedness of the East.

But of course it was not that simple. Khomeini's revolution
was born of those seemingly halcyon days. Even as a child, I
sensed the tensions in the society around me. As I grew older,
I was disturbed in indefinable ways by the totality of Iran's pre-
occupation with the West. The unquestioned belief in the superiority of Americans and Europeans was an insidious, dis-
turbing thread wound through the fabric of my childhood. It
seemed that as a nation we longed for deliverance—from the
boundaries of our lives and traditions as well as from our own
identity. The West was an avenue for change and growth, and
that was good. Yet our love for it was tainted by a corrosive
sense of our own inferiority, rooted in almost a century of ex-

periencing the disdain of the foreigners who came to Iran searching for oil. They wrung obscene concessions from weak and venal Persian kings, then erected separate water fountains for the "natives" toiling in the oilfields.

It went deep, this sense of inferiority. Shopkeepers and restaurateurs serving an American or a Briton often seemed to be trembling on the verge of a kowtow. In government offices, Westerners were quickly ushered to the head of the line. Most of them lived in the expensive houses of North Tehran, houses with pools and pretty gardens. Tehran was full of Americans and Europeans who seemed to take adulation as their due. Many were less educated than some of the Iranians they disdained, yet they were cloaked in subtle arrogance. It came across in their distant smiles, in their patronizing kindnesses ("You speak *such* good English").

The afternoon that a British family came to our door in response to the for-rent ad in *Keyhan International*, I followed a blond, blue-eyed boy around the house, speaking to him in English. I showed him my row of Enid Blyton books, my complete Tarzan of the Apes collection. He stared back at me without a word, eyeing me as if I were surpassingly strange. I showed his mother the faucet at the bottom of the garage that often had water even during the occasional interruptions in our water supply. "Faucet?" she said, looking at me quizzically. "You mean the tap." To this day, I feel diminished by what passed between me and that family, not so much by their aloof condescension as by my eagerness to overcome it.

Yet I knew no other way. As a teenager, the pinnacle of my fantasies saw me transformed into an opulent blonde, whose dark sunglasses and beautiful face stopped traffic. Once, I visited my classmate Behnaz's house, on the second floor of a building that housed her father's pastry shop. I was awed by the wall-to-wall carpeting and cupboards filled with boxes of breakfast cereal. "You put it in milk," Ammeh, my aunt, had explained to me once, when I looked suspiciously at the soggy yellow crumbs floating in her bowl. "Try it. It's good."

When *Charlie's Angels* made its debut, Afsaneh and I refused any family obligation that interfered with watching it. I remember staring for a long time at Jaclyn Smith, pictured in her bikini in our latest issue of *Time* magazine. I studied that pale, slender body as if it belonged to someone of a different species, a species I longed to join.

I can still see her in my mind's eye, her hands steepled in front of her, her eyes looking into mine with a mysterious smile as if to suggest: "I will never reveal to you my essence."

But I knew what it was, this essence. It was the essence of the West.

As a child, the grownups around me used the word *gharb-zadegi* to describe the malady that afflicted our society. It had been coined by the Iranian intellectual Jalal Al-e-Ahmad, who, like many of his peers under the Shah, died in mysterious circumstances. A *gharb-zadeh* was West-struck —as in star-struck or sun-struck. Dazzled to the point of blindness and vertigo.

But when I was twelve, I did not know I suffered from this disequilibirum of the spirit. I just felt inordinately proud of the cherry-red Toyota Baba had imported from Europe when the time came to replace the Ford Mustang—even though the car sat in the garage most of the time. I was secretly in awe of anyone with blonde hair, like the part-Irish classmate I met when I left Iran-Suisse for a new school. When my aunt and uncle decided to send Reza and Mehra to school in England, I was beside myself with envy. Even after Afsaneh and I went to England to keep Ammeh company for a time, and saw my cousins' pinched, unhappy faces at the end of each school day and their tears every morning, I was not deterred. I longed to go back to America even as I had once longed to come home to Iran.

Part of my longing was for movement—I wished to leave the stream for the ocean. I saw America as the promised land, redolent with the smell of rain, exciting and inviting.

But, as much as anything, I wanted to go to America for the status of it. I wanted to move up in the international pecking order. Like so many of the Iranians I knew, I craved deliverance from my own sense of inferiority, both personal and national.

Back then, nothing seemed so appealing as a metamorphosis into the antithesis of myself.

It is only now, some twenty years later, that the realization of my own success hits me like a blow.

ALTHOUGH I was born in Tehran, my roots were in Mashad. As a child, I knew this instinctively. I learned it with the rocking rhythm of the train across the *Kavir* that we rode each spring and summer, breaching the darkness. When morning came at last and the train pulled into the station, it was in my aunts' embrace that I recognized the journey's end.

At Khaleh Farah's house, we would unpack over a tray of tea, my mother and her sisters exchanging news and laughter amid a welter of clothes and presents. For the next few weeks, meals rotated through the houses of our closest relatives. They were all close by, and at night we would walk through the quiet streets of the city on the way home, the children jostling each other playfully, the adults talking and smoking. The streetlights shone on the empty streets, the *Kavir* air was night-cool, and my heart expanded with the joy of being surrounded by family once again.

Each trip to Mashad included a visit to Gonabad, the town where my mother grew up. Most of the family would go, enough that we usually chartered our own bus. I found this a relief, for the bus depot with its diesel fumes and ragged passengers intimidated me. It was full of weathered country folk: leathery crones with toothless gums, snot-faced children with big eyes and matted hair. In our bus I could go about unveiled without worrying about their avid curiosity or their poverty.

The four-hour bus rides were like family parties—the children playing games at the back of the bus, the men talking to the driver up front, the women in between reading the Koran and passing around fruit and cakes. Just when we were beginning to tire of one another and of the emptiness outside our windows, the bus rattled into the tiny green patch that was Gonabad. Here, the streets were tree-shaded, the small center of town giving way to orchards and fields surrounded by seamed walls of mud and straw. My grandfather's house was in the middle of the town, at the base of a shady, dusty alleyway with a greengrocer at the corner. Climbing down from the bus, we would cross the ditch of rushing water that bordered the street, nod hello to the men at the corner standing and clicking their worry beads, and walk down the alley. When the padlock on the wooden door was removed, the two halves fell open with a bang. We left the sunlight of the alley for the dim coolness of the roofed corridor, emerging once again into sunlight in Aghajoon's garden.

His house was built in the traditional style: five rooms opening directly into each other and onto the courtyard—no hallways. At opposite ends of the yard, stone steps led to the outhouse and the kitchen, with its iron door and stone hearth. I put off as long as possible my visit to the outhouse, where a curtain shielded a pit in the ground, and a metal ewer of water, an *aftabeh*, sat next to a dripping faucet. Steppingstones were embedded on either side of the pit, which held shit and buzzing flies. Above, the naked light bulb was festooned with fully inhabited spider webs. Squatting there, I tried hard not to breathe; both fascinated and revolted by this facet of country life.

As much as I hated the facilities at Aghajoon's, I loved the house. Its whitewashed facade rose gracefully over the tiled courtyard and garden, the dome at the center arching over the porch beneath. The high ceilings made it airy and cool inside, and the windows with their bamboo blinds had deep window seats covered with small Persian carpets. The last room was equipped with a *bad-gir*, or "windcatcher," a narrow shaft that connected the chill basement beneath the flagstones to the sunny roof above, generating a constant cool breeze.

As much as I loved the house, I loved the garden more. The moment I stepped into Aghajoon's courtyard, I headed for the deep tiled pool where a blue pump pulled water from an underground cistern. I liked to open the blue metal trapdoor, leaning toward the dark water that reflected my face backlit by sunshine. The stone walkway drew me next, leading me through the vegetable patch, where tiny cherry tomatoes shone bright, past a hedge of almond bushes overshadowed by the apricot trees, and to the other end of the garden. There, just beyond the mud oven where we baked the flat round loaves of country bread, three rooms opened onto the garden. Inside, my grandfather, a doctor, sat at a giant wooden desk, examined patients, and wrote prescriptions. He would smile gently when we ran to him, always willing to dispense a few mouth-watering white tablets of vitamin C.

The house had no running water. We drew our drinking water from the town *ab-anbar*, "water storehouse," and carried it home in earthenware jugs as tall as a child, the jugs, the *kuzeh*s, sweating with moisture and stopped up with a twist of cloth. The *ab-anbar* was in the center of town a short walk from Aghajoon's, beyond a dark archway set in a yellow brick wall. A subtle moisture wafted from the entrance, carried on a breath of chill air. Brick steps led down into damp-scented darkness, ending in a dark pool. The water lapped gently against the bottom step, catching a beam of light from the street above. When we dipped our *kuzeh*s in the cold pool, water gurgled loudly in the silence. It took strength to haul those jugs, now full, up steps slippery with damp. The skin of my face stretched taut again as we rose into dry heat, my eyes blinded by the sunshine.

Back at the house, the *kuzeh*s were propped carefully against the wall in the dim room behind the kitchen. Next door to the kitchen, I would kick my shoes off at the door before entering the carpeted realm of the house. In the parlor, I loved to try to make calls from the old-fashioned telephone, cranking the handle over and over again. In the *bad-gir* room, Homajoon, Khaleh Mina, and Khaleh Farah sat talking over a bowl of the tiny, close-bunched ruby grapes that are a staple of summer in Iran. I took a cluster, searching carefully first for the ladybugs that love the fruit, and ate it lolling against my mother's knee; content in the total absence of a need to be anywhere or do anything.

The only imperative that drove us in Gonabad was the need to eat, and we ate well. The porch was scented all summer long by the sweet, hot scent of apricots, spread out in shallow baskets to dry in the sun. At lunchtime, the women cooked rice in huge iron pots over crackling wood in the kitchen hearth, piling the iron lid with ash and cinders that lent a subtle smokiness to the white grains. They picked herbs and crisp vegetables from the garden, bought eggplant from the corner store, and paid for chickens that were killed as we watched—a gory sight that left me wide-eyed for hours. I had not envisioned the exact fate of the rooster I chased one summer all through the garden, unsuccessfully hunting it for our dinner. Aghajoon's favorite meal was quail. One of his tenant farmers hunted them for him, bringing a brace over every now and then to be plucked and roasted.

The heat of the afternoon was spent in the basement, reached through a metal trapdoor in the flagstones. Once the mattresses were unrolled, my mother and aunts sat talking idly, taking turns tugging the rope attached to the hammock where the newest baby in the family slept. Sometimes they would summon a *band-andaz* and take turns sitting on a chair with their skirts and *chadors* hiked above their knees. The *band-andaz* knelt before them, her practiced fingers sending a crisscross of twine rolling over their exposed legs, plucking swaths of hair in each pass of the string. It looked excruciating, and Afsaneh and I stared incredulously at Homajoon as she reclined at her leisure, chatting with her sisters. "You get used to it," she assured us. "You can't shave! Every hair will grow back tenfold."

When the *band-andaz* left, the talk ceased, and the women rolled themselves in their *chadors* or a *shamad*—a light gauzy covering used in summertime—to sleep. We were expected to nap as well but never dozed as quickly as the grownups seemed to. I liked to lie there in the stillness, surrounded by the sound of quiet breathing. The *shamad* would be soft under my chin, pleasant in the chill that radiated from the stone walls. Sometimes I would lay my face against my mother's veiled form and breathe deeply of her perfume. Eventually my sister would have to jab me awake. While the adults still slept, we collected our cousins, climbed quietly up the stone steps, and pushed open the trapdoor, emerging into total stillness. The sun blazed on the flagstones. The sky was blue. Our hushed voices, our laughter, were the only sounds in that sunlit garden.

Around sunset, the servants spread out the huge Persian carpet in the courtyard. The grownups, still groggy with sleep, drifted out of the house and basement. Those who had procrastinated hurried to make their ablutions and to pray before the sun sank over the horizon. Morning prayers were required to be said before dawn, noon and afternoon prayers before sunset, evening prayers before midnight. Afsaneh and I knew these deadlines well, for whenever we bothered to perform the *namaz* as taught us by Homajoon, we missed them with regularity. In Mashad and Gonabad, peer pressure from our devout relatives often prompted us to renewed effort. When prayers were done, we gathered cross-legged on the carpet for tea and fruit. The last golden rays of light captured us all in a pensive somnolence, but as darkness fell and the bright electric lights blazed, the group became animated once again. Then Baba and Aghajoon played backgammon, with many loud exclamations as the die clicked on the wooden board. We children played our own games, using smooth pebbles in a version of jacks or guessing games that involved hiding one pebble in the fisted hands of a group of players.

On Fridays, my aunts and Homajoon took us for our weekly bath. We walked through the dust of a narrow alley until we reached the public bathhouse, carrying clean clothes in a neatly tied bundle. Habituated to a dearth of water, Iranians bathe less frequently than Americans. As a result, the weekly bath was an elaborate undertaking lasting two or more hours. Once we paid for a cubicle, we would undress and gather in a central tiled area. Here, topless crones with sagging breasts were paid to scrub away dirt and dead skin with the abrasive cloths, the *kiseh*, made for this purpose. My sister and I sat on the wet tiles in the steamy rooms, our bodies swaying back and forth with each jab of the *kiseh*, our faces screwed up in pain. When our skin was raw and pink, we were free to go to our cubicle, which Homajoon disinfected with a noxious purple liquid poured on the tiles. She laid out our clean clothes on top of a sheet of plastic and summoned us in turn into the adjoining room, which held a shower and faucets and tubs for washing clothes. She washed our hair thrice—twice with soap, once with shampoo. Dried and dressed, we emerged at last exhausted and squeaky clean, our wet hair covered by white cotton kerchiefs to keep us from catching cold. Homajoon would reward us with cold orange sodas. Sitting on the chairs outside our cubicle, waiting for Homajoon to finish her own bath, I felt overcome with a pleasant languor. Soda never tasted as good as it did after a visit to the baths; the bottle ice cold against my heated skin, the fizzy liquid sweet and tangy and cold in my throat.

We went home in time for dinner, the whole family gathering in the courtyard once again under a starry sky. Once the dishes had been scrubbed and rinsed and put away, the bedding was brought out. Each family put up their *pasheh-band:* a square tent of mosquito netting attached to trees and nails in the walls by ropes. Afsaneh and I brushed our teeth at the pump, which kept gushing for a full minute after you cranked it—just long enough to rinse. We crawled into our *pasheh-band*, waiting for our parents to join us. The stars were faint through the netting, but cool air circulated through our cocoon. Eventually, silence fell in the garden.

If I got up in the middle of the night for a trip to the outhouse, the brilliance of the stars wheeling above kept me transfixed for long moments. Soon, chilled and awed, I would tiptoe through the ghostly tent city to the one that held my parents and sister. Huddling under my quilt, I slept to the rustling of the wind in the apricot trees, secure in the knowledge that almost everyone I loved was gathered around me in that garden.

IN THE earlier years, when my grandfather was still active, he took us on daily outings to his farms and orchards. We piled into jeeps and rattled through town onto the rutted roads that crisscrossed the fields beyond. We took tin buckets to the orchard at Kalaghabad, "Place of Crows." I remember soft yellow dust gathering in my shoes as I followed a dry streambed to the mud wall that enclosed the fruit trees. Tiny beetles with gray and white stripes crawled on this wall. Inside were plum trees and sticky creepers abloom with huge pink and white flowers. Rows of grapevines grew in little valleys, heavy with bunched green clusters of fruit. At the end were the melons. I remember the sense of wonder I felt the first time I pushed away the dusty leaves of a melon bush to find the fruit nestled beneath, whole and round and perfect.

At one corner of the orchard a pool had been dug, enclosed by mud walls and roofed by the sky. Aghajoon led me there once when I told him I was thirsty. I stared at the still, green water, bees swarming over its surface, and shook my head. Aghajoon, his once-full cheeks already fallen in on either side of a beaked nose, his hair wispy white, looked at me in confusion. He bent stiffly over the pool and brought up water in his cupped hands. "Look, this water is good," he said, holding his hands out to me, water dripping through his fingers. "This water is sweet. What better could you want?"

My favorite place was Kalateh, a little huddle of buildings at the center of acres of fields and orchards. Water from a desert aqueduct flowed across the fields, into a concrete canal, and through a dim hut. There, colas and melons were chilled in the running stream. The stream emptied into a concrete pool so deep it looked black. Here, under the shade of an ancient tree, schools of tiny fish darted, traveling with the stream into the blazing sun, under a mud wall, and into a pond. The pond reflected the whiteness of wide-open space and the tree that leaned over the wall, its surface rippling with the wind that swept across the wheatfields.

There always seemed to be wind blowing across the fields.

The wind tossed the silver leaves on the Russian olive trees, with their rust-colored fruit, and tugged at the black head garments of the village women, who came with brown sun-creased faces and callused hands to pick broom and saffron and pistachios and wheat, each in its season. I walked once with my grandfather down the wide dusty avenue between rows of olive trees, and we passed a group of women carrying their bundles of wheat. Aghajoon led me up to them and paused there for a moment, fingering the grain between thumb and forefinger, his white hair blowing in the wind.

MY GRANDFATHER Abdolrahim Ghassemi was well known in Gonabad. It was not just his thriving medical practice. He was also a prominent landowner, rich not so much in earth but in the water that fed that earth, in the rushing, snow-fed streams that irrigated his acres. Homajoon's mother, who died of leukemia shortly after Afsanch was born, supervised not only her household but the fields. In the few black-and-white photographs that remain of her, I am struck by her presence—which eclipsed her husband's—and her direct and piercing gaze. She bore her husband three girls and two boys. Homajoon was the eldest, her father's favorite. Like most Iranian children then, she called him Aghajoon, dear sir or master. Aghajoon would carry her in front of him on his motorcycle when she was a little girl and leave work to play with her in the garden, where he built mud bricks for her out of matchbox molds and helped her stack them into miniature dwellings.

Homajoon showed early signs of beauty, and the marriage offers began when she was thirteen. By the time she finished school, she was the local belle. The young men of our clan wrote poems to her and courted her at family gatherings. One of them was Khalil Asayesh, a poet and a doctor whose mother was Homajoon's great-aunt. Just finished with his medical studies and two years of mandatory military service, Baba yearned to travel before settling down with a wife. But he worried that if he did, that wife would not be Homa Ghassemi. They married when Homajoon was nineteen and Baba twenty-six.

The ceremony was held in Aghajoon's garden, with the townspeople of Gonabad crowding over the rooftops for a glimpse. Their wedding photograph shows Baba as a drowsy James Dean, his hair already thinning on top, his bride leaning against him draped in white lace. Homajoon looks content and dreamy, with a Mona Lisa smile.

It was a fairytale beginning to a life that was filled with harsh realities. Two months after the wedding, the Shah's soldiers went to the Asayesh house in Mashad and took Baba's father away.

LIKE Aghajoon, my father's father was a prominent man. He, too, was called Aghajan—a more formal variation of Aghajoon. But where Aghajoon was mild, Aghajan was fiery, a man of passionate idealism and strong principle. A mid-level bureaucrat in the Ministry of Finance, Zabihollah Asayesh made his name in politics. After his retirement, he devoted much of his time to the twin struggles that defined Iranian politics for most of the twentieth century, liberation from British and American control and constitutional reform of the monarchy. In Khorasan province, the vast arid state that encompasses most of northeastern Iran, Aghajan was a founder and leader of the Mashad branch of the Iranian Liberation Movement, a group dedicated to democracy and the end of foreign domination in Iran. Since the turn of the century, Britain had controlled Iran's main asset, oil, through its majority stake in the Anglo-Iranian Oil Company. Iran's popular prime minister, Mohammad Mossadegh, nationalized oil in 1951, but he was overthrown in 1953 in a coup engineered by the CIA. America returned the Shah to his throne and replaced Britain as the power behind the throne. The soldiers who took Aghajan away in 1958 had probably been trained by the United States.

They came in the middle of the night. There was loud knocking on the door of Aghajan's house in Mashad, where my parents lived with my grandparents. My hot-tempered father, angry to be roused from sleep, threw a jug of water through the window. Luckily, no one was hurt. They searched the house while Baba's visiting aunt rocked herself and prayed, her thin shoulders hunched beneath her veil, her eyes straying often to the attic above her head. Eventually the soldiers noticed the direction of her frantic glance. When they took my grandfather away, they also took a scrapbook of all of Baba's published poems, hidden in the attic. The scrapbook included three anti-Shah poems printed anonymously in the underground newspaper of the Iranian Communist party, the Hezb-e-Tudeh.

The family passed the night in fear, listening for the sound of soldiers' feet. When they read that scrapbook, they would surely return for Baba.

BABA wrote under the pseudonym Arezoo, a word that means "longing" or "wish." *Who's Who* compilations of Iranian poets still carry his name and picture next to brief snatches of poetry. Arezoo's first poem was published in 1950, when my father was a twenty-year-old medical student. He was just beginning to dabble in politics, drawn despite his father's strong objections into Iran's Communist party.

Baba came by his passion for poetry honestly. His mentor at the time was Aghajan's first cousin Malek al Sho'ara-e-Bahar, the country's premier poet at the time. Bahar, whose honorary title means "King of Poets," encouraged his young relative in both writing and politics. A few years later, Baba published one of his best-known poems, one that resurfaced after the Islamic Revolution.

It was 1953, a turbulent time in modern Iran. The CIA's million-dollar Operation Ajax had just unseated Mossadegh at a cost of only $100,000, clearing the way for Mohammad-Reza Shah Pahlavi's return from exile. The city was in an uproar. The army's Second Armored Division was dispatched to the campus of Tehran University, one of Mossadegh's centers of support. In a classroom of the technical school, three students were gunned down. One of them was an engineering student named Mostafa Bozorgnia, my father's friend and fellow Communist.

Baba called the poem "Machine-gunner" and addressed it to the killers. "Take care," he warned. "Take care not to rest the butt of your machine gun on the dark, damp earth, lest it age or rot away. . . . Take care, for this gun bites, it is rabid, and though today its prey is freedom, one day it will turn against you."

This was one of the poems in the scrapbook the soldiers took away when they came for my grandfather.

IT WAS a time when people went to jail for the crime of not rising for the national anthem, but the soldiers did not return. Someone, Baba speculates, made sure the scrapbook disappeared. One of the monthly social gatherings my father attended in those days included the head of SAVAK, the Shah's U.S.-trained security apparatus. The Communist and the enforcer had shared jokes and drinks. Whatever the reason for my father's continued freedom, Baba has always thought of this man with gratitude.

Baba's only trip to prison was to visit Aghajan, who was held without trial for nearly a year. In exchange for his release, my grandfather promised to abandon his political activity—a promise he fully intended to break. By the time Homajoon was pregnant with me, he was in prison again.

The year was 1961. My parents were living in Tehran, where Baba was now employed at the Ministry of Health. For six months they visited the prison at Ghezel-Ghal'eh, bringing Aghajan home-cooked meals and good wishes and news of the baby on the way.

In 1964 my grandfather was imprisoned for the third and last time. He died at home a year later, when I was three.

Aghajan was sixty-seven years old. His heart and kidneys had failed him. But Baba blamed the prison beatings, the uncertainty, and the heartache of those turbulent years. He blamed the Shah.

DISILLUSIONED with the Communist party's failure to support Mossadegh in the coup of 1953, my father gradually turned from politics. The idealist became a cynic. He channeled his patriotism into the herculean task of inoculating the nation's children against smallpox, fighting a raging cholera epidemic, and bringing medical care to the remote rural corners of the country. Baba rose steadily in the government, although his past activism precluded the lucrative posts of the Shah's inner circle. He stopped publishing poetry and his dreams shifted, revolving now around us, his daughters.

He raised us wholly ignorant of our family's political history. I did not know of Aghajan's trips to prison until I was grown; if I had, I might have better understood Baba's bitterness toward America, the country he nonetheless chose to make his home after we left Iran. Growing up, I absorbed Baba's feelings of patriotism but no hint of criticism of the Shah. My heart would throb when I heard our national anthem: "May our Shahanshah live long . . . for from the grace of the Pahlavis, the land of Iran has come again to the glory of old." I would stand up and salute each time the Shah's face appeared on television, which was often. Only as I grew older, listening to snatches of conversation that ended as soon as I approached, was I checked by vague stirrings of doubt.

I remember sitting in the library at Iran-Suisse one day in sewing class, resenting that the boys got to play soccer while I sat fumbling with a needle. Our teacher glanced negligently at the newspaper while we worked. She was a tall, well-fleshed woman who did everything with a certain indolence. An item caught her eye, and for a moment she was intent. Then she shook her head and sighed. A girl named Goli, who had graduated from Iran-Suisse two years earlier, had been killed in some shooting. Goli had died, said Mrs. Nasiri with extreme disapproval, because of being mixed up with the Wrong People, people who filled her head with Foolish Ideas. I sat up straighter over my uneven embroidery, glad that I wasn't the type of girl to get mixed up with that sort.

Afsaneh and I reacted with disbelief when we saw *Time* magazine's cover issue on torture, for it listed Chile and Iran as the top offenders. "How could this be?" I asked my sister. "It's probably a mistake." Later, I arrived at some fuzzy separation in my mind between the Shah, who was basically pretty good although he had his faults, and SAVAK, the secret police. The Shah was handsome and dapper; his family was clean-cut and looked lovely smiling in their holiday photos, lounging on the beautifully groomed lawn at one of the royal palaces. The crown prince, Reza, was a year my senior and sometimes played soccer with boys I knew. Like many girls my age, I secretly harbored Cinderella dreams of becoming his queen and wished his nose was just a tiny bit smaller.

SAVAK was fear and terror and hushed tales whispered at dinner parties. One relative's husband had disappeared after riding in a taxi with some politically suspect person; another's made a habit of staying behind in Paris when his wife came to Iran for a visit because it was not safe for him to set foot in his own country. And did you hear about the poor Sattaris, Homajoon? Their daughter also has disappeared, poor Mrs. Sattari has no hope . . .

No one knew who might be working for SAVAK. This caused a certain parnoia. Once, on a car trip with my uncle and my family, I made a joke about a dam named for Queen Farah, referring to it as a sewage plant. My family rebuked me, looking around the car as if fearful of detection. I never made a joke at the expense of the royal family again.

In the end, it was my family's history as much as anything that propelled us out of Iran to the United States. Many of the people who ran afoul of SAVAK were young students, people like Goli. What my father once saw as courage he now described, fear edging his voice, as lunacy. He sheltered us from the politics that were once his life's blood. His secret fear was that we would be like him, willing to risk safety and security for an ideal.

Baba was no longer willing to take such risks. He did not want us to end up at Tehran University.

IV · The Break

Tuesday, 21st of Tir, 1356
(July 12th, 1977)

So we ARE going to America. We have plane tickets reserved
for Mordad 22nd, my father was on the phone to Morteza my
uncle only last night; hotel reservations in Paris. We have
our visas and passports, Afsaneh and I. Homa and Khalil
don't yet. We've advertised in Keyhan International *for the*
house and have had several answers. Khalil is under a lot of
pressure arranging everything and consequently irritable.
I just sorted the books, story books I want to take. We're to
pack our cases since we're going to Mashad tomorrow . . .

WHEN I left Iran for the second time, I said good-bye without a backward glance.

I was fifteen years old. I was going to Amrika, which meant
that I no longer needed to envy my classmate Marjan, who
ordered her summer clothes from the Spiegel catalogue, my

cousin Reza, who was attending boarding school in England, or my friend Azadeh, who would be going to school in Switzerland in the fall.

My only regret was leaving a boy I had fallen in love with that summer of 1976. I met him during a vacation on the Caspian shore. We had shared longing looks and one wordless walk on the beach. His family had a villa on the sea; he told me he could predict its moods. As we stood gazing across the tumbled green-gray water, the Soviet Union an invisible landmass beyond, I wondered how that was possible. The night our families' cars went separate ways on the Chalus–Tehran road we were both steeped in silent misery.

Sitting on the plane that would take me from Iran, I stared at the dry horizon and arranged imaginary reunions with him. I was sanguine about a future that would incorporate America without shifting my center of gravity from Iran. Our last trip to America had ended with a reunion in Iran and the resumption of the life I had always known. I had no reason to believe that this trip would be any different.

If I had been an actress in a movie, the music would have signaled the significance of the moment. Somehow I would have known that I stood at the crossroads. Instead I turned away from my mother's tears, my father's tight expression. Even saying good-bye to my aunts did not seem to touch me.

That last day in Mashad, Khaleh Farah knelt in the midst of our belongings scattered through her guest room, wagged her finger at me, and said, "Don't you marry an American. If you marry an American, I won't be your *khaleh* anymore." Her eyes were bright with unshed tears, but I could not give her the reassurance she sought. On a shopping expedition before we left, Khaleh Mina was overcome by weeping. She stood sobbing at the side of the street we waited to cross and asked Afsaneh and me for a promise to remember, a promise to return.

Sixteen-year-old Afsaneh consoled her. I searched for the first break in traffic and hurried across. Standing on the other side, I looked back at my aunt, feeling as if I were already far away.

I did not know how to cope with my family's emotions. I did not understand my own. I did not know, as they did, that this parting might last forever.

WE STAYED in Paris for a few days with my uncle Morteza, who was attending university there. There is a picture of us on the green grounds of Versailles, busy with summer tourists. My family looks morose and disconnected. The camera seems to have captured a heaviness of spirit among us that was in contrast to Dayi Morteza's smiling face. We were shell-shocked, and it showed.

The second plane ride, from Paris to New York, provided both physical and emotional distance from the trauma of leaving Iran. We were able to enter the bright lights of Raleigh-Durham Airport with a stir of excitement. We were returning to Chapel Hill after all, a place of memories, even if many were bad. Our closest friend there was Dr. Vakilzadeh, and he had come to greet us, his smiling face and dapper clothes comfortingly familiar. His sleek and shiny Oldsmobile was as big as a boat, swallowing us up without effort, bags and all.

It was an August night, and the smells and sounds I associated with America assailed me as soon as we left the airport: moisture hanging heavy in the air, the chirp of crickets, the scent of green growth. Homajoon told me to close the window—Dr. Vakilzadeh had the air-conditioning on. It took me a moment to figure out how to obey her, and Afsaneh and I watched with interest as the glass slid silently upward with the press of a button. I sat back against the chill leather, watching billboards flash by. The highway was brightly lit and smooth as silk. Soon road signs advertised the town of Chapel

Hill, the university, the hospital. Before we could reach any of these familiar landmarks, the car left the highway for a wooded, affluent neighborhood at the edge of town. The Vakilzadehs' house was in Lake Forest, though not on the muddy brown lake itself. It stood on the slope of a small hill, surrounded by trees. The car pulled up under a streetlight, and we climbed out. Crossing the fragrant cedar walkway, waiting for the large wooden door to swing open, I felt suddenly hesitant and afraid.

A boy slightly older than I opened the door, welcoming us with a smile and polite greetings. His sister, Dr. Vakilzadeh's wife, Mina, was close behind him. We had last seen Mina-Khanom during a visit to Tehran two years earlier. She greeted us in the foyer with warm embraces and the wide, vivid smile I remembered. Emerging from the perfumed folds of her caftan, Afsaneh and I looked around us with silent awe. The house was like the car, like America itself: shiny and wealthy and new. My eyes took in the mirrors and glossy potted plants, smooth linoleum and gleaming appliances in the kitchen, a lime-green carpet and banks of African violets in the greenhouse off the family room. In the high ceilinged center of the house, a wall of glass revealed a redwood deck overlooking the woods. Nearby, a fountain was silent amid tropical plants. Later, I learned that Mina-Khanom turned it on when she was entertaining. Muted light glowed softly on a big mural, painted in swirling oranges and browns, hanging over the sectional sofa. A baby, wrapped closely in blankets, slept on a burnt-orange ottoman.

I felt dwarfed. My soul shrank within me, expanding a little only when I saw the baby. The Vakilzadehs' new son was the only thing in that room that did not seem alien to me. I gravitated immediately in his direction and sat, taking in the color-scheme of my new life.

WE FOUND a house in Lake Forest on Honeysuckle Road, a long walk from the Vakilzadehs'. Mina-Khanom took us shopping. We bought curved wooden chairs with orange and brown cushions to harmonize with the shag carpet in the family room, a canary-yellow bedspread and matching mural for my parents' bedroom, a glass and chrome dining set for the kitchen. My sister and I had new sheets in bold floral patterns. Homajoon taught us to layer them under thin, fuzzy blankets made of some unnaturally soft synthetic fabric. We were to tuck them in at the base of our new beds. The sheets felt stiff against my skin, and the blankets never seemed to reach quite high enough. I quickly became accustomed to shimmying down in my bed so that I could stay warm. I never questioned that I had to make whatever adjustments were necessary to fit in this new life.

When September rolled around, Afsaneh was swallowed up on the verdant, teeming campus of the University of North Carolina. An orange bus peopled with strange, unfriendly faces took me to Chapel Hill High School. High school American style was an endless series of shocks to my system. Used to standing up when the teacher walked into class, I marveled at the casual, dismissive attitude of my classmates. They chewed gum in class. They put their legs up on the desks. They seemed wholly unconstrained by the conventions familiar to me.

On the bus, I shuddered inwardly the first time a quiet, blonde girl named Lisa, irritated over some minor issue, said the word "shit." I concluded that, contrary to appearances, she must not be a good girl. Profanity was a stranger to my vocabulary. In the cafeteria, I was shocked when I saw my classmate Samantha sit on a boy's lap. In the hallway I saw a boy and girl entwined next to their lockers, kissing deeply, and felt rocked to my core.

It didn't matter that this second time in America I spoke English. If anything, my extensive vocabulary contributed to making me an outcast. I did not understand about fitting in, I did not know what it meant to be cool. I wore the wrong clothes—nylon knee-highs under my denim skirt, plain tops that revealed none of the fashion sense my classmates prized. I was earnest instead of nonchalant, jumping out of the bus to extinguish a smoking cigarette stub so that it wouldn't start a fire. My classmates drove cars on screeching tires and boasted of getting drunk on the weekends. As teenagers, they had done and seen things I would not have done and seen in a lifetime spent in Iran. I could not believe that in America children were allowed to drive, let alone partake of all those other unspeakables—sex and drugs and alcohol.

But in America childhood seemed to end early, to be replaced by a cultivated cynicism that masked both vulnerability and immaturity. I was still a child, with a child's joy in simple pleasures and a secret delight in the safety of rules and restrictions. Going to high school in America felt like a violation of my childhood, an abrupt and painful loss of innocence.

I waited for the bus each day with anxiety knotting my stomach, resolving that today I would break through the wall that seemed to separate me from my classmates. I came home each afternoon, having failed, and sedated myself with endless episodes of *M*A*S*H* and *Gilligan's Island*. If I saw one of my classmates at the mall on the weekends, I walked the other way. The one Iranian I knew at school seemed to want nothing to do with me—he had been where I was not too long before, and he had no desire to go back. My closest friends were the characters on the television screen, Hawkeye and Radar and Gilligan. They were the only Americans I knew who seemed friendly and unthreatening.

My family fared no better. To this day, we do not talk of

those first years in America. We do not acknowledge how they shaped us into what we are today. When a natural disaster hits, people talk for years about the height of the waves, the ferocity of the wind, the power of the earth tremor that remade the landscape of their lives. But the emotional disasters in our lives go largely unacknowledged, their repercussions unclaimed.

My family was wrenched from all that was loved and familiar, yet there were no rituals to mourn our loss, no baptism for the painful rebirth. Instead, we were driven to bury the evidence of our personal cataclysm. Our differentness was a taint that we carried. The consuming need to belong led us to purge ourselves of that which once made us who we were—our accents, our awkward clothes, our beliefs.

We were faced with an unspoken choice: to be alienated from the world around us or from our innermost selves.

WHEN we first moved to Chapel Hill, we saw America as an interlude in our Iranian lives. Homajoon and Baba planned to stay in North Carolina for a year, maybe two—just to see us settled, my father told us. Then they would return. After college—so the scenario went, although here my father's eyes showed fear and his words became overemphatic—we girls would return to Iran. We would get a Western education and put it to good use—in Iran.

We held on to that scenario long after we suspected in our hearts that there would be no return. We could not admit to ourselves that we had left it all behind for good—the house, the mountains, the people, the country we claimed as our own. Baba had been raised on the mantra of loving and serving Iran; he had tried to instill those values in us. As so often when one's choices diverge from one's beliefs, it was easier just to paper over the gap. So we continued to use the Iranian calendar. We ended long-distance phone conversations with the promise to 'visit—soon. We began sentences with the phrase: "When we go back."

At first, we continously juxtaposed our new life against the old. Iran was our primary frame of reference; America was full of oddities. In America, diners salted their watermelon instead of their oranges. People wore torn clothes in the grocery store. Men tied their hair in ponytails. Women smoked in public. The streetlights carried a deep yellow tint; so did the vanilla ice cream. The faces in the supermarket, the mall, the classroom seemed pale and bland, somehow indistinguishable from one another.

Sometime during that first year we were overcome by the futility of holding on to the past. Iran was far away. My sister and I were misfits in school, my parents were heartsick and beleaguered and suddenly a liability to their children, who longed to be absolved of the complexities of heritage. Piece by piece, we started letting go of the old and embracing the new. I bought a pair of rust-colored corduroys. My sister acquired, amid great family tension, a boyfriend. Homajoon started cultivating African violets. Baba unbent enough to venture outdoors in flipflops instead of proper shoes.

In time we became American in more substantial ways, in habits of thought and speech and expectation. By 1979, when I started college, the feeling of being a foreigner, that churning nausea fed by fear and isolation, had begun to subside. The yellow tone of the streetlights, the taste of salted butter, the weekend trips to the mall, had become familiar. We kept our faces turned forward, and one day we crossed an invisible line so that when we looked back at the world we had left behind, it was across a widening gulf of space, time, and culture.

For years I felt powerless to bridge this gulf. At my first newspaper job after college, friends told me with approval that

I was "well adjusted," "Americanized." They could not see the Iranian in me. But with each year I became more aware of an inner schism. Deep inside, I could not forget that I began life as an Iranian.

In 1990, when I obtained the green card that cemented my foothold in the West and permitted travel to and from Iran, it was instinct that drove me to return. With that first trip back, I began the long, slow road toward resurrecting a buried self. And vowed I would never suffer that inner shriveling of an isolated core, the immigrant's small death, again.

WE HAD been in America for more than a year when the Shah of Iran lost his throne.

It was a day my father had longed for. For years, the Pahlavis had been to Iranian advocates of democracy what the men who sent tanks into Tiananmen Square were to the Chinese. But when the soldiers gunned down the three Tehran University students in 1953 and Baba wrote his poem, he did not expect it to prove prophetic. To anyone living under the Shah, the end of the Pahlavis seemed inconceivable. Few people had even heard of Ayatollah Khomeini; he had spent more than a decade in exile, first in Turkey, then Iraq, and later in France. Long an opponent of the Shah, Khomeini was exiled in 1964 after he vociferously opposed the Shah's approval of political immunity for U.S. forces stationed in Iran.

But in 1978 the guns were indeed turned against the soldiers, and Khomeini returned from exile. Baba was amazed and exultant. He paced the living room of our house in Chapel Hill in his pajamas, hovering between tears and laughter. "Let's pack our bags," he said. "Let's go home."

I was only sixteen at the time, but I knew he didn't mean it. Poor Baba; life had carried him a long way from those early days of poetry and politics. Long ago, he had chosen to look after his family and leave the causes of his youth to others. That road brought him to an American living room decorated in peach and orange, where he stayed up late at night studying for an endless series of medical certification exams, conscious that his competitors were young men and women fresh out of medical school. Mehdi Bazargan, appointed prime minister by Khomeini, had once been part of Baba's political circle. Back in Iran, the magazines of the revolution were reprinting my father's poem "The Machine-gunner." History was in the making, and Baba had once been a part of it, but no more. Instead, he got to share the moment of his dreams with a couple of teenage girls who were embarrassed by his emotion. All we wanted was to change the channel.

Instead of packing, Baba had to return to his studying. In the morning, he got up to go to work in the small office at the Carolina Population Center where he conducted research—a far cry from his suite in Tehran with its accouterments of power and prestige. On the weekend, we went to the mall. The mundane routines of this life so far from Iran sapped Baba's ardor, soaking it up like white bread absorbing gravy. When we talked of Iran, we spoke of how unsettled the situation was, how dangerous, and how—as a high official in the Pahlavi regime—Baba might be subject to reprisals from the new government. Sitting together in our cozy living room, we watched the revolution unfold in stark television images and switched it off each night with a click of the remote control.

It was just as well. For Bazargan soon lost his post, and his followers, the educated upper class who had for so long worked against the Shah, were pushed aside. Prominent men, including men Baba had worked with and admired, were summarily executed. Women were restricted, first in dress, then in other freedoms. The light in Baba's eyes was replaced by incalculable bitterness. In time, he arrived at a sort of comfortable detachment—easily achieved when Iran was an ocean away. At parties in Chapel Hill or Raleigh or Durham, where the men discussed politics over drinks while the women talked of roses and violets, Baba would inevitably conclude with a cynical comment. Even after my sister and I finished college, there were the vagaries of the Islamic regime and the war with Iraq to cite as obstacles to our return.

Looking back, I see the truth that we evaded then. Iran could have been stable and at peace; we would still have stayed in America.

The reasons for this are not wholly clear to me. The mythology says that people like myself come to this country seeking freedom. There is certainly truth to that statement. What troubles me is that the desire to live in a democracy is not, I suspect, our primary motive. We are lured by the promise of gas grills and dishwashers, three television sets per household, multiplex theaters showing new releases, blue jeans and Nikes and ninety-nine channels including MTV. I often read my daughter the story of the Three Billy Goats Gruff, who braved the troll under the river bridge so that they could leave their rocky hillside for the green grass of the meadow. They grew fat and happy on the other side of the river. That is why most of us come to America, I think; the grass is greener and we want to grow fat and happy. But I, like my father, am an idealist. I believe there should be more to life than our natural human urge to find better grazing ground.

I see my own absurdity, trying to fathom the rhymes and reasons of decisions long past. After all, we did not sit on a mountaintop and contemplate the path we were taking. It evolved in increments, shaped through the layered accumulation of moments. It is only in hindsight that I try to pick out a pattern, seeking to come to terms with the past. From this vantage point, I can see that we stayed in America because it offered us a better life. We stayed, too, because we had endured much in leaving Iran, and it would have been too hard to go back.

But most of all we stayed, I think, because we had changed, like an animal that, adapting to a new habitat, is no longer suited to the old.

My aunts were right to weep that last day in Mashad, as if saying good-bye for the last time. They knew what we only suspected, that once we left Iran, America would claim us, and there would be no going back.

AT THE glass and chrome kitchen table on Honeysuckle Road, Baba held weekend lectures. "I want to talk to you," he would say to Afsaneh and me, and our hearts would sink. We would eat our pita bread and cheese and jam and eggs without our usual gusto. Homajoon would sip her tea silently, looking down at the table, rubbing fiercely at a stain on the glass now and then, her face drawn and sad. My sister and I dreaded these talks, not only because they were virtual monologues, lasting for at least an hour, but because they focused on uncomfortable topics. Like a preacher on his pulpit, Baba would try to impress on us two things: one, the importance of going back to Iran; and two, the importance of retaining our identity. This latter topic was littered with references to the iniquities of Western culture. Baba told us early and often that there is only one thing American boys want from girls: bed. His face was twisted in distaste as he said this, for he is the product of a puritanical culture. Like most parents, he was also acutely uncomfortable discussing sex with his daughters. In Iran, it would not have been an issue. But now my sister and I were living in a moral jungle, rampant with sex, drugs, and alcohol. My parents lived in fear that we would fall prey to these dangers.

Afsaneh and I were in no risk of succumbing to drugs or al-

cohol—we were far too strait-laced, too centered in our family
life. Boys, though, were a different matter. Baba's views
seemed, at best, extreme. Although I had no desire for the way
of life of my classmates, which seemed shiftless and sordid, I
wanted to flirt and dance and talk with boys. In Iran, this
would have been the stuff of adolescence, weathered with an
argument or two or three. In America, where the social boundaries are so much broader, my interest in the opposite sex was
like a fuse connected to a powder keg.

I was not allowed to "date" boys. Dating was a wholly foreign concept to me, because it removed young people from the
family context that reigned supreme in Iran. In Westernized
Tehran, we may have gone to a movie with a boy, but we lived
our lives in a context shaped by adults. Here, teenagers seemed
to live in their own parallel universe in which they made the
rules. To me, it looked like anarchy. I had no interest in trading
my world for theirs. But if by some fluke some boy someday
asked me to go to Purdy's, the teenage disco on Franklin Street
that my classmates raved about, I wanted to be able to say yes.

It was 1978. I was a junior in high school, well into my second year in the United States. Still an outcast, I had formed my
own tenuous connections—primarily with other outcasts. We
started a badminton club; it included myself, a Chinese student who spoke barely any English, an Indonesian girl who
fared somewhat better, and two American girls who were too
warmhearted to disdain our company. My efforts to tutor my
fellow foreigners prompted the school counselor to nominate
me for the National Honor Society. My interest in my English
classes led to my writing for the school newspaper. I was still
on the social fringe, but I no longer crept through the hallways
like a frightened fawn. I had learned how to pretend non-
chalance.

My fragile confidence changed the way others responded to

me. Suddenly, the mantle of invisibility I had worn since I came to America seemed to lift. Boys started to notice me once again. I started spending lunch hours with a tall, curly-haired classmate named Doug. Once, to Homajoon's horror, he came by the house. I received him with a mixture of anxiety and delight. We talked on the porch; I was afraid to invite him in. In Iran, Homajoon would have asked Doug to take a seat and served him fruit and drinks. He would have been the family's guest, not mine. Here in America, though, there was that parallel world. It made it possible for Doug to visit me without acknowledging my mother. Neither Homajoon nor I knew what to do.

In the spring, Doug asked me to the prom. It was a family crisis of the quiet kind—no shouting, just a pall hanging over the house compounded of my guilt and longing and my parents' fear and dismay. After much deliberation, my father decided that I could go—he did not want me to feel deprived, he said. My parents' permission should have lightened the atmosphere, but it had the opposite effect. Baba looked grim all the time. My mother wore the resigned, grieving look of someone absorbing a mortal blow. Afsaneh did her best to blend into the background.

Homajoon took me shopping for a new dress, a swishy pale rose gown that came to my feet and looked suitably promlike. Under a pretext, we borrowed a black shawl from Mina Vakilzadeh. My mother was horrified that our Iranian friends might learn that I was going out with a boy, never thinking that they were far better acquainted with the concept than she. As for our family in Iran—we all knew that my aunts could never catch wind of this transgression. The knowledge of how shocked they would be weighed heavily on my parents. Like me, they were caught between two irreconcilable cultures.

In the days leading up to the prom, I vacillated between

misery and excitement. I tried hard not to betray my feelings, seeking instinctively to downplay the occasion in front of my parents. I was tormented by two great anxieties. What were my parents thinking behind their bleak faces? And would I make a fool of myself in front of my classmates? I wanted desperately to seize this chance to belong; but I was venturing into uncharted territory. "Prom" was a new word in my vocabulary. I had to call a friend to find out what a corsage was and what I was supposed to do with one. I was sixteen years old, but I had never been alone with a boy before.

When Doug came to pick me up that Saturday night in May, I wasted no time in saying good-bye to my parents. I wanted to reassure them, but it was beyond my power. Instead, I walked out of the house, feeling a great weight slip from my shoulders. In the car, Doug showed me the flask he carried in the breast pocket of his tuxedo. I eyed it with disapproval, refusing when he offered me a sip. We had dinner at a restaurant just outside town, the Slugs at the Pines, where other overdressed teenagers mingled with the middle-aged. Then we were driving up the lonely road to the high school, walking into the gymnasium that was decorated for Chapel Hill High's Junior/Senior Prom.

I retain a confused recollection of bright lights and loud voices, my classmates reeling about with overbright eyes, faces gleaming with makeup and sweat. My fragile confidence evaporated in the beat of the disco lights. I felt like a child once again as I saw the couples around me dancing, exchanging deeply sexual kisses. We sat on the bleachers and watched, and Doug slipped his arm around my shoulders. I stiffened and pulled away, avoiding his eyes. When we danced, he held me in his arms and tried to kiss me. I ducked and turned my cheek. I knew I was violating the rules as he knew them. I knew I had been allowed to bend my parents' rules with the unspoken understanding that I would not break them. I felt trapped by who I was, what I was. I longed fiercely, suddenly, miserably, to be free—free to belong in the world that was now mine.

That night, the web of belief and expectation that bound me broke apart and formed a new pattern. I slipped the tight moorings of my heritage and began to yield to the imperative of the here and now.

I remember the precise moment it happened. It was toward the end of the evening, after a few moments spent outside in the cool night air. We were walking back into the gymnasium, and Doug swung an arm around my shoulder.

This time I did not pull away. Casually, as if I had done this thousands of times before, I let my own arm come up and settle gingerly around his waist. It was as far as I was prepared to go, a tiny shift in my narrow boundaries. Even so, I trembled at my own daring.

I can still remember, as if it were seared into the palm of my hand, the cool silk of his jacket, the forbidden heat of the body beneath.

I can still remember the moment when I let go of that girl from Iran.

V · The Gulf

London, Ontario, Canada
August 1985

M Y MOTHER comes forward sleepy-eyed, opening her arms to hold me. Afsaneh and her husband, Ali, are right behind her. Baba hoists the suitcases from the elevator and we all stand there in the hallway of my parents' high-rise condominium, exchanging hugs and excited greetings. It is the first time in more than a year that my sister and I have been able to coordinate our visits to Canada. Afsaneh and Ali flew here from Raleigh, where my sister is a design consultant. I came from Miami, where I am a reporter for the *Miami Herald*. "Let's go inside," Homajoon urges, glancing down the deserted hallway anxiously. "You'll wake the neighbors."

Once inside, I look around expectantly, but the door to the guest bedroom is closed. Khaleh Farah and Afzal are already asleep.

I prowl through the apartment, seeking proof of the presence of these visitors from the past. In the guest bathroom, I stand gazing at a pair of worn brown rubber slippers, the kind men and boys in Iran wear to run to buy bread from the corner bakery. Two toothbrushes in a glass, the bristles thin and flattened with wear. An old-fashioned shaving brush with only a few flakes of paint left on the smooth wood. A tube of Paveh toothpaste, the words written in English on one side, Farsi on the other. A box of razor blades with a familiar alligator on the cover and the label Nacet. I turn the word over in my mouth, tasting it, shaping it with my tongue, summoning dim memories of a time when it was one of the innumerable household phrases that defined the day-to-day rituals of my life. The spare belongings of our visitors from Iran stand out sharply against the modern Plexiglas shelf, all acluster in an island as if to protect their fragile modesty in this immodest land.

In the kitchen, we gather around the familiar glass and chrome table, speaking in hushed voices. My mother brings out two blouses she has bought for my sister and me. Both have long sleeves and high necks. "You chose these so we would look *eslami*, didn't you?" I say accusingly.

Homajoon laughs, looking slightly guilty. "Khaleh Farah has gotten so *eslami*," she says. "She keeps her head covered even in front of your father."

I am amazed. Khaleh Farah has known Baba as long as my mother has, for more than a quarter of a century. My father and Afzal are like brothers. Growing up, during our family visits to Mashad, we would all wear veils in certain parts of town and on visits to the shrine of Imam Reza. But in Tehran, Khaleh Farah would stay in our house and go about the city unveiled.

I ask, "Have you had any arguments?"

"Almost had one tonight," Homajoon says. "She said one of the good things about the Islamic Republic is that now everyone is veiled. I said as a matter of fact I think that's one of the bad things." (It was funny to hear this from my mother, whom I grew up seeing as the blind defender of rules and traditions. She was the one who, nervously—because she was afraid of my response—asked me not to bring shorts or sleeveless clothes on this visit. She was surprised and pleased when I didn't make a fuss.)

Last question. The most important one. "Do she and Afzal still have their sense of humor?"

Homajoon starts laughing, reminded of one of Khaleh Farah's wry comments. My mother, starting to bake my favorite cake at midnight, forgot to put in the flour. Khaleh Farah came into the kitchen and asked, "Sister, how is your omelette?"

GETTING ready for bed that night, I look around with appreciation, drinking in the touches of home: the familiar peach-toned living room set, the bright canvases my sister painted as a teenager at the University of North Carolina at Chapel Hill, the fresh flowers my mother buys each time we visit. Homajoon's plants fill every nook and cranny, orchids and violets, ivy and jade plants, philodendron and ferns.

More than four years have passed since the day I watched my parents, perched in the high cab of a Ryder truck, pull out of town and my daily life forever. My father's face was grim as he sat behind the steering wheel. Baba's pride was broken, chunked into odds and ends of furniture and books and household appliances, all of it packed into the yellow truck he was to drive to Winnipeg, in the Canadian west. The United States had no place for him—not economically, as a new yet no longer young resident of psychiatry, and not politically, as a would-be immigrant whose only chance of winning a green card was to seek political asylum. This was something Baba refused to do, for it meant turning his back on Iran.

All those nights poring over medical texts after the long day's work, napping under the dining table so he wouldn't get too comfortable, then resuming his studies. All those exams, which he failed seven times before finally winning the right to practice medicine in America. All those blows to his identity endured without complaint. And it came to this, an ignominious departure from a country that would not have him.

I looked at Homajoon, pale and wan beside Baba. She wore the look of dumb suffering that I had learned to recognize in our years in America. If Baba's identity had been fractured by the years in Chapel Hill, hers had been dismantled. Cut off from her career by visa restrictions, cut off from her sisters and brothers, Homajoon's world had narrowed down to her responsibilities as the mother of daughters who were reluctant to be mothered. Now that, too, was at an end. She would have her empty nest in a cold city of strangers, many miles from everyone and everything she had ever valued.

They had driven to see me in Winston-Salem, where I worked that summer as an intern at the afternoon newspaper. We said our good-byes in a mall parking lot. There was no way to redeem the moment. I stood on the sidewalk and watched the truck drive away. My parents had never seemed so alone, so vulnerable. My heart contracted with fear and grief. Yet I also felt a furtive sense of exultation, a tainted delight in finally attaining—at my parents' expense—the independence my American peers took for granted.

In the mysterious way of life, my parents' departure from North Carolina, their darkest moment since leaving Iran, was also the beginning of a bright new chapter in their lives. In Canada, where immigrants were not the problem they had become in the United States, and where the Iranian hostage crisis was not a personal affront, my parents felt welcome in a way they had not in America. Winnipeg offered a warm and friendly Iranian community, which embraced Homajoon and Baba with delight. My parents rented a cozy condominium, and Baba started work at a nearby hospital. Back in Chapel

Hill, Baba's friends had said he was crazy to study psychiatry when his Iranian medical degree was in general medicine. But my father had always wanted to be a psychiatrist. In Canada this dream came true at last. Canada offered my parents what the United States never had: the promise of permanence. This was a balm to hearts that had endured too many partings.

Living in Canada had two major drawbacks, however. One was the ferocious winters. Homajoon and Baba bought big down coats that covered them from head to toe and learned their way through the underground warrens peculiar to cold cities: malls and offices and restaurants linked by miles of heated passageways. They came to enjoy lamenting the weather. "The temperature is forty below, counting wind chill," Homajoon would report to me triumphantly over the phone. "The rivers are frozen." When they moved to London, a town in eastern Canada near Toronto, the winters seemed balmy in comparison.

Canada's other major drawback was harder to remedy. My parents left Iran to be with their daughters. Now we lived in different countries, and they could not reconcile themselves to the distance. I spent every school vacation in Canada. Once I graduated and started work, it was the same. The hours passed slowly during those vacations, especially in the winter. Even so, I was glad to go home to my parents whenever possible. These visits gave me an anchor, something I had come to need desperately.

When we lived together in Chapel Hill, I took for granted the sense of connection my parents offered. My days as a college student overshadowed the Iranian side of my life—family parties, letters from Mashad, Baba's failed attempts to get me to read books in Farsi. In those years, being Iranian was an obstacle, a shackle, a guilt trip. My relationship with my parents revolved around painful arguments over boyfriends and curfews. Our views were as irreconcilable as the two cultures we advocated for. It took my parents' move to Canada to bring about a truce.

Once my parents left, there was nothing to prevent me from embracing the lifestyle of my peers, and American culture seemed to swallow me up whole. By the time I graduated from UNC, my metamorphosis was complete. Moving to Miami to start my first job, I was consumed by the competitive, hard-edged world of journalism. Reporting on life in a violent, divided city, I struggled to make sense of gritty realities that had hitherto been beyond my scope.

That first summer at the *Miami Herald*, my job included keeping track of the murders that happened almost daily, a total included in stories reporting each new murder. When I started work in 1983, the Mariel boatlift was recent history, and drug wars and crooked cops and body parts floating in Biscayne Bay provided ample grist for the journalist's mill. The murder tally was kept on a large piece of posterboard tacked on the wall of the police room, a dingy space where I was to monitor the babbling of a dozen police and fire department scanners. That year, there were well over three hundred murders. I boasted of living in the country's murder capital, affecting the unconcern that was expected of me in that hard-bitten newsroom. But the truth was that nothing in my sheltered existence had prepared me for what I read about, what I wrote about, and what I saw in those years.

The day I was dispatched to the litter-strewn cemetery off Biscayne Boulevard, I was armored with my journalistic poise. Someone had found a body, the city editor told me. I stood outside the yellow crime tape, taking notes as a police officer described the incident. A tourist had been walking on Biscayne Boulevard. A man snatched his briefcase. The tourist followed. Searching the bushes for his stolen property, this visitor to sunny Florida found instead a dead woman.

The tourist was nowhere to be found. I had been at the *Her-*

ald long enough to know that settling for what the cops were willing to give me would not do. Uncertain of what I hoped to accomplish, my heart pounding at the prospect of a clash with authority, I surreptitiously worked my way into the bushes beyond the crime tape. No one saw me. The officers were busy with the body.

The body in the red shirt. The face bloated. The eyes bulging, bloodshot and lidless. She had been in the bushes for a while.

Back at the office, I wrote two paragraphs that ran, without a byline, on the obituary page. Her name was Karen Hicks, she was nineteen.

Once her death had been noted on the murder tally, it was forgotten. But the experience haunted me. At night, lying in bed in the silent apartment I shared with a largely absent roommate, I was overwhelmed by the sense of being alone in a cruel world. Cut off from family and friends, I felt myself adrift. There were no buffers between me and life's harsh realities, no cocoon of familiarity and routine to shelter me, no one's love to anchor me.

When I was in high school and college, I longed to be delivered of the burdens of the past, to be free to belong in the world of my peers. Now that I lived outside the constraints of family and culture, I discovered in myself a need to belong in ways that transcended the superficial acceptance of my friends.

By the summer of 1985, when I went home to Canada to greet the aunt and uncle I had loved throughout childhood, I had discovered a need to belong to myself.

IN THE morning I sleep late. I can hear their voices, already at breakfast. I listen for Khaleh Farah's familiar tones, alternately gruff and humorous, and Afzal's infectious guffaw. Sneaking into the bathroom for a shower, I take more care than usual getting dressed. It has been eight years since I left Iran. In that time, only Homajoon has returned to visit. For the rest of us, Khaleh Farah and Afzal's journey to Canada is the first bridge across the great divide that opened with our immigration to America.

I walk up behind them at the breakfast table. Khaleh Farah sits wrapped in her white house veil. At her side, Afzal seems to be wearing the same plaid flannel shirt he wore eight years ago. He has never cared about material things, I remember, my heart welling with love and gratitude—gratitude that in this respect, at least, he is unchanged. I say something in greeting, and suddenly we are holding each other, my *khaleh* and I, holding tight as if we will never let go. Afzal, the unemotional one, grasps my hand and squeezes hard, his eyes damp. My parents, Afsaneh, and Ali watch silently. I can feel the tears in my mother's eyes.

I sit down at the table. The intensity of the moment yields to everyday conversation. But as I eat, as I speak, Khaleh Farah and Afzal are both studying my face.

I know what they are looking for: to see how much of me is still theirs and not America's.

THE days pass too quickly. They pass too slowly. I'm all torn up inside. I talk to Khaleh Farah, and first on her agenda is God, religion, and prayer. She tells me, with a determined sort of hopefulness, that she brought me a prayer veil from Iran.

It hurts to tell her that I don't pray anymore. I remember vividly my mother telling me a year ago, "I told Khaleh Farah you pray and it was like you'd given her the world." I remember how, as soon as was humanly possible, they had sent me a *janamaz*, the prayer rug, along with a silk cloth holding the cool gray holy stone, the *mohr*.

I prayed for a while in the privacy of my bedroom in Miami. It didn't work. I still wonder if it's worth trying to preserve culture and ritual in a vacuum.

I try to atone by showing Khaleh Farah that I'm open to religion. I discuss *namaz* with her, hoping against hope that she will infuse me with enough faith to ward off the chill of my disconnected urban life. But she's too dogmatic, too intent on converting me.

Khaleh Farah stands at the ironing table, her hair covered with a scarf, as always, pressing the full-length navy tunic she has brought to wear outside the house in place of a veil. She tells me the same sort of things they taught in my religion classes in school in Tehran.

Namaz is like a clear brook in which you purify yourself. It keeps you clean and gives you serenity. *Namaz* is the only way to worship God.

I feel overcome with claustrophobia. I feel as though my aunt's piercing eyes are judging me, and the verdict is that I'm a wanderer from the one true path, corrupted by my environment, that—most fearful thought of all—I am not Iranian enough. That is my own inner fear, that here in the heat of American life, my identity is wisping away from me.

I am convulsed by the contradictions of my life, straddling a fissure between two worlds that are immeasurably distant. My mind is always whispering for me to find a more stable spot. Pick one side or the other. Pick one world or the other.

I lean sometimes this way, sometimes that. Here in my parents' home, Iran is as tangible as my mother standing at the kitchen table. It is as though Homajoon and Baba breathe their identity, the accumulation of their life and experience, into any space they occupy anywhere in the world, and Iran resonates through it all.

Back in Miami, my life is indistinguishable from that of any young American professional. I go to work, eat a lot of pizza, make costly forays to the malls on weekends. I struggle to get ahead and calculate the likely amount of my next raise.

I can carry on for months that way, oblivious of any inner

dissonance, as though I've forgotten the cool summer nights out on the porch when my aunts would tell me stories and the scent of jasmine perfumed the air.

Until one day I wake up feeling bereft, as though I let the strings of a beloved kite slip through my fingers and it is now only a speck in the distance.

Here with my aunt, the Farsi words taste strange in my mouth. And I am standing on the other side of a great gulf, looking across at my Khaleh Farah, whom I love but cannot reach.

SHE came, she tells me, because of *Seleh-ye-Arham*. "Do you know what *Seleh-ye-Arham* is, Gel-gel-jan?" she asks, tugging at my heart with her use of the childhood nickname. I shake my head. "*Seleh-y-Arham* means 'ties of the womb,'" Khaleh Farah says. Family ties are sacred, and in God's eyes it is incumbent on the faithful to preserve them. And that's why she came, leaving behind her three children, the youngest a girl of twelve.

She tells me about making the pilgrimage to Mecca last year. The *hajj*, the pilgrimage to the Ka'aba or House of God in Saudi Arabia's holy city, is mandatory for all Muslims who can afford to go. But this was Khaleh Farah's first *hajj*. "So much holiness," she tells me, her face radiating awe. "There's the House of God plunked down in the middle of this barren desert. There are thousands and thousands of pilgrims, and everyone turns toward the House of God to pray. It's a trip everyone should make. Afzal, with all his traveling, hasn't made the one trip that's really necessary."

She and Afzal are going to go together in 1989, she tells me. They've already paid the government 52,000 tomans to save them a place on that pilgrimage. That's half of what a teacher in Iran makes in a year.

I ask her if she still plans to send her sons to Canada for university. "Our boys can't leave now," she says, distressed. "It's war." Young men in Iran must serve a two-year stint in the military even in peacetime.

But I can tell she hasn't abandoned this dream; I see it in her obsessive concern with the cost of things here. With every exclamation of dismay, she is measuring, considering. "Even if the boys could come," she says, "we'd never be able to afford paying for them one year, let alone more."

We're standing on an escalator that spans the three floors of Eaton Centre, a mammoth shopping mall in downtown Toronto, where Khaleh Farah is self-conscious about the stares she attracts with her navy blue head scarf, tunic, and pants. As the escalator rises, she takes in the scene beneath her: the colorful decorations, bright lights, teeming shoppers, and countless stores, each like a treasure box. She pays silent homage for a moment to this monument of Western supremacy, her worry eclipsed by a burst of awe. "I wish the kids were here," she says.

The escalator reaches the top. Once she has carefully made the transition from stair to floor, she says, "You all will have to save your money and help us. Maybe we can compensate by buying you something over there, like gold." She looks at me anxiously. "Yes," I say, hiding my dismay. We move on, and I have to make a conscious effort to stay at her side. Walking in Khaleh Farah's company keeps me from blending into the crowd; it robs me of the anonymity it took me so long to achieve in the West.

I step closer to her and take her hand in mine.

AT NIGHT I lie in bed writing in my journal, trying to make sense of my disordered thoughts. I left the ordeal of work and urban problems in Miami in search of a vacation. Instead, I find myself plunged into a maelstrom of conflicting emotions. I want to run away from Khaleh Farah, from what she makes me see, from what she makes me feel. It is as though she has opened the Pandora's box where, at long last, I had succeeded in burying all the pain and fear and confusion born of our move to America. I left home for a new land, I was miserable as so many immigrants are, and now it's behind me—this is the myth I wish to hold on to. Khaleh Farah's visit is shattering the myth, and with it the foundation of my new life. She reminds me of the gulf between my two worlds and that it must somehow be my task to bridge it.

Her watchful tallying of sins and dollars, the way her eyes seem constantly to juxtapose my world with the one she knows, is a wave of reproof sweeping before her. "Finish the food on your plate," she tells me, much as she did when I was a child. I try to obey, my resentment layered with guilt. "America is the root of all evil," she says. "Look at this war. It's no laughing matter. The young men don't come back at all or come back with limbs missing. All those Iraqi atrocities, and the world never said a word."

I do not wish to acknowledge that the United States, through its support of Saddam Hussein, is waging war on Iran. By her very presence, Khaleh Farah calls into question every aspect of my life: the country where I choose to live, the apartment by the bay where I come and go as I please, the lack of any place in my so-secular life for God or charity, the way I take for granted the abundance of everything, from electricity to meat to all the pretty things in the stores.

I wonder for the hundredth time what separates me, so wealthy in things and opportunities, from my old friend Elham, who has been in prison for three years now and has arthritis at twenty-three. When I knew her, Elham had long brown hair and a ready smile, a warm heart, and a budding sense of justice that landed her in the Mujahedeen-e-Khalq, a group seeking to depose the mullahs.

In a different way, I think Khaleh Farah is asking herself the same question. There is a strange sense of tears just beneath the surface, of out-of-placeness about her. We're sitting in my parents' plush green Oldsmobile, driving to Toronto for the day. The sky is blue, afloat with white puffs of cloud. The countryside is green. Khaleh Farah's careworn hand rests on my knee as she comments on the beauty of the landscape. I can feel her spirit stirring, stretching awake.

Then she starts talking of the war as if under some inner compulsion. Mass funerals every Monday and Thursday in Mashad. One week, there were four hundred dead. "Four hundred," she says. "That's the size of a high school class. One day it's Reza's classmate, another Ramin's, another the neighbor's . . . How can anyone have good spirits and think and do for oneself when every day these things are going on?"

The green velvety car seat is hot from the sun. The cool air blows in through the open window, clean and sweet. I look up at her sitting next to me and see that the blue sky has made Khaleh Farah cry. A bright tear rolls down her cheek. Everyone is silent. From the front seat Afzal says, at last, "All right now, let's enjoy the scenery."

Khaleh Farah looks out the window and wipes away the tear with a finger. "How green it is here," she says. "How waterless is Iran."

THAT night in bed, I am remembering my geography lessons in fourth grade, the maps we drew, the way we had to memorize each country's main products. I used to feel envy because the map of Europe was green and that of Iran was, except for one verdant strip along the Caspian Sea, yellow and brown. In history classes we studied maps again, and with each century I felt a pang as the boundaries of Iran shrank, dwindling steadily from the zenith of the glory days so often evoked by the Shah, when the Persian Empire rivaled that of the Romans. I remember the resentment I felt looking at a modern map of Iran crouched under the vast bulk of the U.S.S.R., noticing what a tiny slice of the huge Caspian Sea belonged to my country, the rest of it falling within the Soviet Union.

I don't notice things like that anymore.

KHALEH Farah has stopped asking me if I want to pray. But right before sunset, when it's time for evening *namaz*, she says wistfully, without looking at me "In Iran the *mo'azzin* would be chanting the call to prayer just about now. And everyone drops what they're doing and goes to pray."

I roll my eyes, but inwardly, I am afraid. It seems that religion has swallowed whole the Khaleh Farah I once knew, blunting her astringent personality with a sense of resignation. It is as though now that she has committed to the true path, all that is left is to wait for the next world and sigh this one away. Whatever God wills.

Later I realize that God's will is merely a ballast in the turbulence of her life. One day toward the end of my stay, the phone rings and Khaleh Farah is summoned to the kitchen to take the call. Moments later, she puts down the receiver and walks toward me with tears in her eyes and arms outstretched, saying, "Gel-gel-jan, our boy has passed."

My cousin Reza, who is graduating from high school this year, won't have to go to the Iraqi front. He has passed the *concours*, the exam that decides which fortunate youths will go to university. She tells me that only 44,000 passed of the 450,000 who took the test.

All day she's bubbling over, suddenly free of that troublesome sense of resignation. "He's made a very high ranking, the rascal," she says.

"He'll be able to get into any university he chooses," my brother-in-law Ali says, smiling. Khaleh Farah's eyes brim with happy tears. She laughs suddenly. "He wants Calvin Klein jeans for a present. And a windbreaker. I'm afraid they'll kick him out of university for being so trendy."

"Calvin Klein jeans are the most expensive," Ali tells her, well aware of how carefully my aunt has to budget her purchases.

"They cost about forty dollars," I add.

Khaleh Farah sighs. "I'll have to get them for him now that he's passed," she says.

"How is everyone else?" I ask. She sighs again, thinking of her two sons and daughter home in Mashad. "They're fine," she says. "Maryam had trouble finding the fried onions. I told her where they were."

That night, when Baba and Afzal pull out the backgammon set after dinner and their hearty laughter warms the small apartment, I'm visited by memories of the old days, when a score of my relatives would sit down to each meal and half a dozen little cousins were always underfoot, begging for a piece of gum or a playmate. In those days no one ever dreamed we'd never be together in the same house again.

I've never asked my parents if they'll go back to Iran one day. I am afraid to, afraid to question the quality of change. How it sweeps across your life, forever altering its contours. How it whistles like the wind in empty rooms in one's heart. I do not want to yield to change, to acknowledge that the little cousins are all grown now and I may never care enough to do what it would take to see them again. I do not wish to acknowledge that I have relinquished my claim on Iran, that it is here that I know the streets and intersections, the newest songs on the radio.

AFTER the first flush of our reunion, I often find myself treating my *khaleh* with cool distance. I cannot help it, even though I see the uncertainty in her eyes each time she looks into mine, trying to decode the messages she sees there, searching for one that speaks to her of lasting love, of a love that can bridge the gulf between us. I feel this love, but it is locked away behind the barriers that separate us, barriers born of too many years spent living in different worlds.

But the weeks dissolve our mutual unease. It is two nights before my return to Miami, at one in the morning. My aunt Shahin and her husband are visiting from Toronto, where they are thinking of settling. With them are their sons, my childhood playmates Reza and Mehra. The apartment is small, so Khaleh Farah and I share the living room. She insists on taking the floor. Her makeshift bed is laid out next to my couch, but she can't sleep, still excited by her son's success in the *concours*. We talk in the darkness, me lying on the couch with my cheek propped on one hand, she sitting cross-legged with her veil draped loosely about her, her fingers moving restlessly on her worry beads. Everyone else is in the kitchen, playing cards. I can see her face by the thread of light from beneath the closed door.

"I made a *nazr* if Reza should pass the concours," she says. "When I go back, I'll have to fulfill it."

What kind of vow? I ask her. *Nazr-e-Imam Hossein*, she tells me, explaining traditions I never had a chance to learn. You vow to hold a feast for thirty or forty friends and relatives. Everything on the table has to be green like the martyr Hossein's flag. Hossein, grandson of the Prophet Mohammad, is one of the Shi'ites' greatest heroes. Khaleh Farah made all kinds of vows for Reza's *concours*—five hundred tomans to charity if he passed, double that amount if he passed with a high enough score to enter medical school.

She tells me about all the vows she has made on our behalf. For my father, when he sat for the Canadian medical boards.

For my mother, when she was in the hospital last year. For my sister and me when we bought cars. "The custom is to spill blood so no blood shall be spilled," she explains.

"How many sheep have you slaughtered over the years?" I ask her. A memory stirs in my mind: a dirty, woolly animal led into our garage in Tehran by the equally ragged executioner, the stomach-clenching smell of boiled mutton, men and women with pinched faces lining up in the dusty alley to receive the bowls of cooked meat.

"A lot," Khaleh Farah answers. "Maybe two a year. When they parceled out the meat the last time, fights nearly broke out among those who wanted more." She sighs. "It's been so long people haven't had meat."

Each Ramadan, she tells me, she gives money to the poor as part of another vow. "It's a special *nazr* to keep you safe," she tells me. "It equals the price of three kilos of bread."

I am ashamed and comforted at the thought of the silent, constant solicitude that has been directed my way all these years from across the sea. I wish I had ways so laden in meaning, so anchored in tradition, to give voice to my love and concern for the people who are absent from my life except in memory.

Khaleh Farah tells me a story about a man she saw in a store once in Mashad. He was bitter and belligerent, you could tell something was wrong with him. Being Khaleh Farah, she said, "Sir, there seems to be something troubling you. What is it?" He told her, "You'd be like this, too, if you had my problems. I had five children. I lived in Ahwaz. I lost my home and four of my children in the war."

He told her he had moved to Mashad, far away from the Iraqi border, with his wife and remaining child. He said he bought a house in one of the villages nearby.

"I said, 'Why live in the villages, why not live in the city?'"

Khaleh Farah recalls. "He said, 'I'm afraid my one child will get run over by a car.'

"I said, 'Whatever is God's will.'"

We are both silent.

"Goodnight, Gel-Gel-jan," she says.

"Goodnight, Khaleh Farah."

Miami, Florida
September 2, 1985

KHALEH Farah returns to Iran tomorrow.

When I spoke to her on the phone to say good-bye, her voice was choked with tears. I started to cry, too, fighting to control my grief.

Forgive me for upsetting you, she said.

Miami, Florida
October 7, 1985

I'VE HAD Khaleh Farah's letter for two weeks now. It lies unopened on my desk.

I do not want to hear what she has to say to me. What can there be to say except futile expressions of affection and longing?

Her letter can't bridge the gap between us. It is a frail voice that echoes and is quickly lost, emphasizing the emptiness.

VI · Homecoming: Iran

Mashad
October 22, 1992

KHALEH Farah answers the phone when it rings in the morning. She hangs up full of excitement. A friend is going to Gonabad. He has agreed to haul an oil stove and a drum of fuel so they will be there when we visit.

My aunt bustles into the yard, my cousin Maryam and I in her wake. Soon Khaleh Farah is clambering over the piles of odds and ends in the storage shed next to the outdoor toilet, trying to get at the big old stove. We help her drag it out, getting coated with dust from the overhanging leaves of the fig tree in the process. Maryam goes into the house for a rag to wipe the stove. I stand waiting for her by the steps. I notice that the chicken cage is empty. "What happened to the chicken?" I ask Maryam when she comes back, rag in hand. "That poor chicken, it didn't lay an egg for just one day and Qamar wrung its neck," she says, her mouth quirking with humor.

At lunch, we have chicken in a savory tomato stew. "Is this your chicken?" I ask Khaleh Farah. She laughs. "That one was too old," she says. "It's in the freezer. We'll have it someday when it's just us, no guests."

KHALEH Mina summons me to the bathhouse for a discreet conference. She has installed a *farangi* (foreign) toilet in her *hammam* next to the shower. The Iranian toilet, the ceramic hole in the ground, is in a separate cubicle of the suite.

My aunt wants to know where to put the roll of toilet paper she holds gingerly in both hands. In Iran, people wash themselves after going to to the bathroom, using the metal or plastic *aftabeh*s filled with water or a small hose installed for the purpose. They consider the concept of toilet paper unhygienic and un-Islamic. ("But we shower every day," I said to Khaleh Farah when she expressed herself on the topic during her visit to Canada. "Unwashed butts," she muttered in response.)

I look around. There is no toilet paper holder, of course. "How about here?" I suggest, pointing to the back of the commode.

"Thank you," says Khaleh Mina. Her eyes are twinkling. "You see, we don't know these things, *khaleh*," she says apologetically.

Later that day I reach for the toilet paper. It is soggy and wet. Someone has recently taken a shower.

We devise a new system: the toilet paper will be kept inside a plastic bag.

Mashad
October 26, 1992

WE GO to the shrine of Imam Reza in the late afternoon to hear the drums and the trumpets. They sound at sunrise, sunset, and whenever the Imam heals someone. I am too lazy to go at sunrise, and it is not possible to foresee a miracle, so it must be sunset.

It is a crisp autumn day, and the *haram* is not as crowded as it is in summer. It takes Afzal minutes to find a parking space. We wait for him to padlock the steering wheel as a precaution against theft, my aunts fussing with my *chador*. Bibi stands next to them, watching with a smile. Bibi, who married Agha-joon after my grandmother died, now spends her days raising her widowed daughter's two children. Her daughter, Vida, works as a teacher and had the morning shift today, so Bibi was able to get away for this visit to the shrine.

We walk briskly into the maze of surrounding courtyards, heading for the #2 Family Shoe Locker, where men and women are permitted to enter together. "They've divided the *haram* into men's sections and women's sections," Khaleh Farah tells me with a snort of displeasure. "God's house has nothing to do with whether you're a man or a woman."

We hand our shoes to the attendant. Khaleh Farah carefully puts away the slip he gives her and we step across the threshold. In the women's section my aunts and Bibi quickly find prayer stones and finish their *namaz*. Even so, the sky is pink by the time we rendezvous with Afzal in the main courtyard. Pigeons roost on the golden dome of a water house fitted with rows of faucets. Nearby, the metal grillework of the Imam's tomb is visible. The ground next to it is covered with bedding, the men and women reclining on their mattresses in two separate sections. This is where the desperately ill come, waiting for the Imam to work his healing miracles. The grille above their heads is festooned with tokens of hope and prayer—bits of string, fluttering ribbons, pieces of twine, a padlock. I watch a woman working her way back across the sea of bedding, her tearful face twisted with misery.

Suddenly a hush descends on the courtyard. High above, in the balcony of the minarets, I see movement. A long trumpet is briefly outlined against the sky, like the kind pictured in tales of heraldry. Then it begins, a haunting, rousing call of drums and trumpets resounding through the courtyard, ushering the sun over the horizon. It goes on and on for fifteen minutes, a twisting melody, both militant and poignant, catching at my heart, making me want to laugh and cry and fight and pray.

The last note dies away. Khaleh Mina is weeping softly. Khaleh Farah wipes her eyes with a corner of her veil and smiles at me triumphantly. I find it hard to speak, but the expression on my face seems to satisfy her.

Just as we turn to leave, there is a stir at one end of the courtyard. The crowd parts before a group of men in black shirts and tunics bearing a coffin on their shoulders. They set it down and stand around it in two rows, chanting koranic verse. These are the *sineh-zans*, the "chest-beaters," hired to mourn at the funerals of top clergy and other important folk. Watching their rhythmic movements and bearded faces, I am suddenly very much aware of the cotton of my favorite shirt, a striped button-down from the Limited, against my skin. The jeans hugging my hips seem to be a symbol of the close embrace of the West. This physical reminder of my connection with another world reassures me, providing a counterpoint to the ritual unfolding before my eyes.

I remember how frightened I was years ago, as a child, watching a cavalcade of *sineh-zans* march through our alleyway during the month of Muharram. Now that I live far away, I can listen to the Arabic chant and appreciate its rhythms. I accept, with a sense of inner yielding, that this passionate ritual, this pulsing vein of religious zeal, is my birthright. It is part of who I am.

I will not deny it.

I am quiet on the way back to the car, wishing I could stick my hands in my pockets.

FROM prayer we turn our attention to shopping, Afzal leaving us to go home for more substantive pursuits. After an hour of browsing the gold-sellers' quarter next to the shrine, we catch a cab home. The four of us squeeze into the backseat rather than share space with the male driver. I listen to my aunts and Bibi talk. "My colleague's husband died last night," Khaleh Mina is saying. "I have to say the *namaz Laylat-o-dafn* for him tonight."

Bibi and Khaleh Farah perk up. "Oh, no. You're supposed to say that prayer after the funeral," Bibi says.

"I don't think so," Khaleh Mina answers. Her nose is still red from weeping at the shrine, but her eyes are bright with interest. "It must be said between the *maghrib* [sunset] and the *esha* [evening] prayer. And I think I need to do it tonight."

Khaleh Farah joins in with her opinion, and they happily debate the issue all the way home.

October 27, 1992

I AM at war with my aunts, my father—everyone, it seems, except my cousin Ali. He is the only one who is not aghast at the idea of my driving alone to Gonabad. Or if he is, he is willing to lend me his car nonetheless. "A woman alone!" my aunts twitter. "It's not safe. You should have a man with you."

I glare at them, offended. "I've been driving alone for years, in far more dangerous circumstances," I say. I'm wasting my breath. Their opposition is organic and immovable. What I propose is just not done.

I complain to Baba, expecting support, when he makes his

regularly scheduled phone call from Toronto. My father has never been one to hold my sister and me back—certainly not on the grounds that we are female. But I had forgotten about his blind spot—his fatherly instincts melded with the Iranian code of chivalry that demands that men protect women. "Are you crazy?" he says. "You're being stubborn, as usual. It's not safe."

After I hang up, Khaleh Farah looks up at me apprehensively. "Did Dr. Asayesh give his permission?" she asks, hoping Baba has succeeded where she's failed.

"I don't need anyone's permission." I answer so furiously that my aunt looks miserable. "I'm an adult. Being a woman doesn't change that."

The night before the trip I pack my bag. My aunts' tactics have shifted. My cousin Ali is drafted to sit beside me while I drive his car to Gonabad. I won't have it. "Good for you," Ali's sister Laleh says to me. I look at her with gratitude. "They try to put us in a cage, Laleh," I say. "We've got to shake them up."

I ask Khaleh Farah and Khaleh Mina to come with me as my passengers. "It'll be so much faster than the bus," I say. "It'll be fun." They decline politely. "I don't trust passenger cars, *khaleh*," Khaleh Mina says to me. "You see how people drive on these roads? They're like animals. I feel safer in the bus."

So it is that on Thursday morning Khaleh Farah, muttering prayers, holds a tray bearing the Koran over my head. I pass under it, kiss the holy book and her, and drive off with a wave. My first mission is to find a gas station—not a simple thing, since gas is sold at only a handful of government pumping stations. Ramin spent a half-hour giving me directions, but I get lost anyway. My map of Mashad is useless because the street names keep changing. I manage to find my way to the dusty highway heading south and drive through a haze of diesel fumes, surrounded on every side by trucks and buses.

At the gas station just outside Mashad, the attendant looks at me with a knowing leer. Fortunately, I still remember how to deal with this kind of treatment. I turn away haughtily, prepared to wait in line. Instead, he waves me on to the open pump ahead of the other cars. I give him an abbreviated smile and look fixedly in the opposite direction while he pumps the gas.

In open desert at last, I give myself up to a sense of total exhilaration. To be alone is wonderful. To be independent, briefly in charge of my own fate, is even better. To enjoy these blessings in the bosom of my family in Iran is a miracle.

The sun beats down warmly from a cloudless sky. The open window catches a lot of dust but also the cool breeze. I watch the speedometer carefully. Ali's car is eleven years old and doesn't do well at speeds higher than fifty miles an hour. Each time I reach a hill, I hold my breath as the little white Renault labors upward, praying that it doesn't break down in the middle of the desert and show me up in front of my aunts.

I drive through miles of flat, dun-colored country, the mountains looming in the distance. The sense of bleakness is heightened by the occasional industrial installation, a brick or salt factory or military camp. The small settlements I pass through offer quick splashes of color—piles of orange tangerines and yellow-green winter melons, a testament to the hidden fertility of this harsh land.

After three hours I am feeling the tedium. On the side of the road, I notice a bus pulled over on the shoulder. Just past it, three black-veiled women, like a small flock of crows, lean beckoning toward the road. *Chadori* hitchhikers? Hardly. As I whiz by, I realize with a jolt that I have just passed my aunts and Aghdas Khanom, Ali's mother. I pull over quickly and back up. The three women walk slowly to meet me, holding their veils above ankles stockinged in thick beige nylon. I climb out to greet them, worried. "What happened?" I ask, embracing each in turn.

"The bus broke down," Khaleh Mina says.

My jaw drops. I start hooting with laughter. "That's wonderful!" I say. "I told you so."

My aunts are laughing too. Aghdas-jan cracks a slow smile. "Well, come on," I say. "I'm so glad I saw you. Get in the car."

"We're glad we saw you too," Khaleh Mina says, her eyes twinkling. "I see this lady zooming by, just hitting the gas pedal, and I say, 'Can that be Gel-gel-jan?'"

I laugh with her. "I wasn't going that fast."

"You go on, *khaleh*," Khaleh Mina says. "We'll stay with the bus. They're fixing it already."

"Are you sure?" I ask.

"Go ahead and open the house," Khaleh Farah says. "We won't be too far behind you."

I embrace them again and watch them walk back to the bus, black veils flapping in the wind.

Back in the car, I can't wipe the smile off my face. God is good.

AGH Abdollah has come to pay his respects. He sits on the porch, his white turban a contrast to his sunburned face, his lean body bent forward, elbows on knees, staring across the garden. I sit next to him, keeping him company until my aunts arrive.

For two years I have exchanged polite greetings with this man, my mother's relative and our caretaker here in Gonabad. But I have yet to know what to say to him. For all his devotion to our family, he seems to have nothing to say to me.

But this year is to be different. Agh Abdollah clears his throat. I wait eagerly.

"In America, is meat expensive?" he asks.

Caught off guard, I stare blankly for a moment. But I am determined to seize this conversational opening. I do some rapid calculations in my head and throw out a number, praying that it will do.

He is pleased, for it turns out that meat is much cheaper in Iran.

"It's much better quality, too," I say, trying to prolong our exchange. "We never get lamb there, just beef."

Agh Abdollah has nothing to say to this. We go back to staring at the garden, waiting for my aunts.

Tehran
November 1992

FROM Elham's house, we take a cab north into the foothills of the Alburz mountains. As we approach Jamaran, the streets become narrow and empty. The leaves on the sparse trees are golden. We pass the occasional dry goods store, a dry cleaner's, the hospital that was built when Ayatollah Khomeini moved here from the holy city of Qom. His doctor recommended the cleaner air of the mountains after a heart attack. At last we arrive at the house, just down the street from the modest mosque where the Imam sat on a balcony and waved a limp, tired hand at the masses below, his image broadcast around an incredulous world.

The house is small and nondescript except for the revolutionary guards who still protect it. They are polite, humble young men, a refreshing change from so many of their peers across the city. I produce my letter from the Ministry of Islamic Guidance, which oversees the activities of newspaper reporters. While we wait, I look around the tiny garden, peering through sliding glass doors at two rooms containing a bed, a couch, a bookcase, and a telephone. From here, Khomeini

challenged the West. From here, he made the decision to prolong the war with Iraq. From here, he left for the hospital
where he drew his last breath, the whole world waiting to hear
that he was, indeed, dead.

Soon, an old man in a vest, shirt, and pajama pants is climbing laboriously up the steps. Haj Issa Jafari bows in greeting as
I introduce myself and my friend. He was the Imam's servant,
he tells us. He looks curiously from me to Elham. We are both
veiled, but Elham wears her flowing black *chador* as if it were
a part of her. "It's like a badge of support for the revolution,"
she told me in the cab coming here. I spent most of the time
stealing covert glances at her, trying to reconcile this dedi
cated fundamentalist with the girl who flirted with the boys
in the schoolyard of Iran-Suisse, with the intrepid woman who
joined the Mujahedeen, with the prisoner who spent four years
in a cell block. A few moments later, when the Haji starts
showing us around, I hear Elham sniffling. I look at her and see
that she is wiping away tears. "Why are you crying?" I murmur. "Well, I loved him a lot," she says of the man whose minions sent her to prison.

The Haji looks at her approvingly and continues the tour.
"This is where they would sit," he says, referring to his master
in the plural, out of both courtesy and awe. "These are their
shoes. The people would sit over here."

I look at these scant relics of Khomeini's life intently, as
if they can reveal to me the mystery of the man. Khomeini,
the uncompromising voice of conscience raised for decades
against the Shah. Khomeini, the leader of the revolution,
whose return to Tehran in February 1979 marked the end of
more than two thousand years of Iranian monarchy. Khomeini, the zealot, who urged mothers, during the bloodbaths
of the early 1980s, to turn their children in if they opposed the
regime. Khomeini, the ascetic, who was mourned as far away

as Rockville, Maryland, because, as one Indian woman told me, he had restored pride to Islam.

"Two or three thousand people a day came from all over the country to see the master," the Haji is saying. Clerics just graduated from the seminary came to receive their turbans from his hands. Scholars came to confer with him. Couples came to have him inscribe their marriage contract. Many came just to kiss his hand.

"You see, the Imam had a love that was something else," the Haji says. "Because, after centuries, suddenly a light shone from the heavens that illuminated the whole world. It was something like that. Because Islam was about to be destroyed."

He shows us the carpeted room next to the bedroom. "This is where they waited," Haji says. "When the holy Imam rang, they could go in. Khamenei. Rafsanjani. Ardabili. All the leaders. Every day the master would listen to the eight o'clock news, then call them in."

He tells us his master's schedule ("He did not waste a minute of the day"): prayer, the study of the Koran, the work of the nation, meals at the adjoining house of his wife, visits with his beloved grandchildren, naps, and daily walks. "When he was walking around the garden, he would do three things at once," Haji says. "He had his radio in his hand, listening to the news. He had his worry beads in the other, saying the name of God. And he was walking."

The old man disappears for a while, returning with a tray of tea. He sits on the carpet in the room where the leaders of Iran waited to speak with the Imam. Elham and I sit beside him, taking the tiny glasses of tea in their saucers with a word of thanks. Haji is telling us how he fell and hurt his neck, trying to collect persimmons from the top branches of the tree in the garden. He strapped two ladders together to reach those branches because the Imam could not tolerate waste, he says.

He talks for a long time of his master's final day on earth, telling it like an epic tale. By the end, his eyes are shining with tears. "Tell the world," he says to me, looking as if he wishes to trust me but cannot be sure. "Tell all humanity."

Then he glances through the window at the sky and says: "It's time for prayer, and I'm keeping you here."

Elham quickly takes the cue. "We've delayed you," she says. "Please, go ahead and pray, we'll wait." She turns to me, explaining as if I might not understand: "It's important to him to say his prayers promptly."

She asks the Haji for a *mohr* so that she can pray as well. The old man walks to a ledge in the wall. "Please help yourself," he says, lifting a bundle from the shelf. "Here is a *janamaz*. Whenever Ahmad-Agha visits he uses it."

Elham's eyes widen at this mention of Khomeini's son, an *ayatollah* himself. "This is Ahmad-Agha's *janamaz*?" she asks, awestruck. Haji nods, spreads it for her, and collects the tea things. "We've put you to so much trouble," I say. "It's my pleasure," Haji answers. "You just tell all this to the world."

I watch Elham pray, her black veil obscuring her face, the colorful red and blue prayer rug beneath her feet, the cloth for the *mohr* embroidered silver on black. I think about following her example, but it feels like hypocrisy. I sit on the edge of the couch instead. My camera hangs heavily around my neck, giving me the distance I seek.

NIGHT has fallen. We walk along the narrow street next to a gully of rushing water that gleams faintly in the darkness. The neighborhood is suffering one of Tehran's frequent power outages, and oil lamps glow from the dim interiors of the stores we pass. Just as we are wondering how to get home, a driver gives us a ride to a nearby thoroughfare. "Here you can get a cab or a bus into the city," he says. He refuses to take our money.

Elham leads me to the bus stop, her veil flapping in the

breeze. I climb into the smelly vehicle behind her. The driver jerks his head toward the back of the bus, the women's section. I sit down with a sigh of relief, glad I wore my veil to Jamaran. Even so, when we stopped by the mosque where Khomeini preached, the women who politely searched my bag could see that I was not of them. My lack of faith was as visible to them as their devotion was to me. I could see it in their direct and guileless gaze, in the humbleness of their bearing. It made me feel small, as if they trod a higher path.

I shake off these fancies and turn to Elham. The interior of the bus is illuminated, and in its yellow glow I can see my friend clearly, the piercing dark eyes, the long, strongly marked eyebrows. I am remembering when I first met her, in Chapel Hill. Her parents were studying there, just as mine were. They lived in university housing, as we did. We played blindman's buff in the room she shared with her sister, their prison-striped bunk beds identical to the one Afsaneh and I shared. When her family returned to Iran shortly after we did, Elham came to Iran-Suisse. She was an instant hit among my classmates, with her long hair and slim grace and the touch of American sophistication that had somehow eluded me. Though we were the same age, she always seemed older—perhaps because she was the oldest of three children, used to responsibility.

Our paths separated when my family returned to America. I heard that she organized demonstrations at school, that she had joined the Mujahedeen, that she was on the run. When I was in college, she was in prison. When I was working for the *Baltimore Sun*, she was enrolled in university in Ahwaz, struggling to make up for lost time. She is a medical student now, close to attaining her first year of residency. It is a wonderful achievement, but her family rarely mentions it. The well-traveled, educated parents, the beautiful sister, the young brother with his skeptical eyes, seem subtly distanced from Elham. Elham and her black veil stand out in a household that is as Western as any I have seen. But it was not the family that changed, it was Elham.

Our school friends look at me askance when I mention her name. They nod with polite skepticism when I suggest that her conversion from enemy of the revolution to its ardent follower is genuine. They do not seem to find any mystery, as I do, in the way Elham's passionate idealism changed direction.

Now, on the bus, I find the courage to ask how it happened.

Elham seems happy to talk about it. "When I went to prison, I expected to instantly go to the torture chamber," she tells me. "Instead, they picked me up at two P.M. and I sat there until eleven at night. Then they took me to a room and talked to me. It's true that it was prison, but in reality I came out of bondage. I had time to think."

She decided the ideals of the Mujahedeen were an illusion, she says. The group had no tolerance for dissent; members were not even allowed to read or watch Iranian newscasts on the grounds that they were propaganda.

"When did you come to believe in the government?" I ask.

"It wasn't one particular point in time," she says. "It happened gradually."

The bus pulls to a stop. Elham hurries to the front to pay. "How many?" the driver asks. "Two," she tells him. She ends the transaction with brisk efficiency as I trail in her wake. We descend into a brightly lit square where merchants are hawking bananas, colorful sweaters, lighting fixtures, and bolts of fabric. Our paths part here. "I'm going to Khomeini's tomb on Friday," I say. "Do you want to come?"

She does. I watch her disappear into the crowd, a black form swallowed up by so many others.

THE next day, I am invited to lunch at the home of a friend. Bijan and his wife greet me cordially, and we sit down around the wooden dining table, the room lit by mild sunshine filtered through autumn leaves. Halfway through the salad, I mention my visit to Jamaran, speaking with admiration of the aura of simplicity and faith that clings to the place. Before I know it, I am embroiled in a furious debate with Bijan about the sins and virtues of the Islamic regime. He is so upset, his face is red. I go to bed that night with my stomach churning, feeling poisoned by the unrelenting hostility my secular friends feel toward the orthodox Iranians who run the country today. The fact that I don't unequivocally reject the mullahs' Iran means that I am seen as something of a Neville Chamberlain among my peers. I have to struggle not to apologize for stating what seems to be an innocuous fact—that despite its documented excesses, despite its totalitarianism, despite its policing of private lives, the Islamic Republic of Iran has its good points.

I go over them as I lie in bed, reviewing the case I made so unsuccessfully at lunch today. It's true that candidates for parliament are limited to the religiously orthodox, but at least power is distributed among many. This government is more accountable than the Shah's. As much as I resent enforced *hejab*, it still reflects the beliefs of a majority of men and women in my country. Even though censorship is common, I find reassuring the openness with which people criticize the government at home and in public. I love the new Iranian cinema, which has a vibrant originality that was missing in the days when we counted the hours until the arrival of the latest James Bond movie. Despite the obstacles to creative freedom that drive so many Iranian artists to leave the country, it seems to me that the official rejection of Western imports has created room for authentically Iranian culture to blossom. I think it's splendid that carpet weaving is offered as a major at universities and that smoking is no longer allowed on airplanes. I admire the handful of female representatives in parliament and their efforts to improve the status of women—even though all are fundamentalists, with views far removed from mine. I am impressed with Tehran's can-do mayor, a cleric and an intellectual both, who is changing the face of the city with his trees and flowers and light fixtures. (He also levies huge taxes, earning the enmity of many Tehranis. In a few years, he will be convicted in a sensational, controversial trial for bribery and corruption.)

Bijan responded with recitations—all true—of what is wrong in Iran. Corruption and thuggery. Primitive executions. Crushing bureaucracy. Conspicuous consumption among the supposedly religious elite. An emphasis on orthodoxy at the expense of merit.

It takes me a long time to understand the emotional intensity Bijan brings to our debate. His bitterness, his cynicism, his refusal to consider other points of view, spring from a well of human pain. Having lived through the revolution's bloody early years, he cannot dismiss them as lightly as I tend to. Since the ascent of the mullahs, he and his kind have been marginalized, dethroned, and robbed of their sense of belonging. The alienation among the former elite is profound, a cancer that eats at the fabric of Iranian society. "Our problem, unfortunately, is that we are at war with everything that has come about after the revolution," he tells me later, when both of us have calmed down. "As a result, we miss out on a lot of things."

The dispossession of some of Iran's best and brightest costs the country in every way. But when I was growing up, another, larger group of Iranians felt like strangers in their own land. I am reminded of this when a worshiper at the tomb of Khomeini says to me, "It was no good in the old days. Why, I remember walking down Lalehzar Street and seeing a woman in a *sundress*." He pauses to let the impact of his words sink in.

His relatives, sitting around him on a carpeted dais, shake
their heads in disbelief and disapproval. I am sure this man's
grandmother, mother, and wife never dreamed of giving up the
veil or, with it, the traditions and beliefs of centuries. In his
eyes, I see what this sight, so commonplace to me, meant to
him. I glimpse his sense of violation, of a country turned up-
side down.

The Shah embraced the West and rejected Islam. The mullahs have done the reverse. My country is a house divided, and
people like me, who seek a middle ground, must pay the price.

Yet for all my attempt at objectivity, I know in my heart
that I have my own emotional agenda. Beneath my rational
opinions lurks an urge toward advocacy every bit as intense as
Bijan's. I seek to minimize the dark side of Iran because I am
afraid. If Iran is as dreadful as he says, what is there for me to
come back to? After so many years of being divorced from my
heritage, where will I be if I find it not worth claiming?

I need to embrace Iran. Bijan needs to reject it.

For I am the one who chooses to live across the sea, free to
love a country that can no longer cost me. And he is the one
who stays, paying the price each day for what is wrong in Iran.

AT ELHAM'S suggestion, we take a cab to the south end of
town and a bus from there. As we rattle through the fumes of
South Tehran, Elham is telling me about Khomeini's funeral.
She was among the masses who followed the coffin in a spec-
tacle that seemed bizarre to the Western world. "You just
wanted to do it," Elham says. "I was upset. It was like *Ashura*
[the most important Shi'ite day of mourning, when Imam
Hossein was murdered]. All these people, beating their chests.
A lot of people were walking barefoot."

"Walking barefoot?" I ask. "Why?"

"It was symbolic," Elham says. "People do the same kinds

of things for movie stars. Like, what value is there to movie stars?"

I want her to decode for me her love for Khomeini, but she shakes her head helplessly. "I can't say I loved him for these reasons, here's one and here's two," Elham says. "Whatever I say can't do justice to it. It's like anyone you love. Like if someone asks why do you love your mother, what can you say? Do you know what I mean?"

We're in the *kavir* now, barren except for a lone water tower and a field of stubby pines, just planted and dusty. "Greenbelt Plan," a city sign proclaims. At least they're trying, I think to myself. In the distant haze, a gold dome and minarets rise from the desert. Khomeini's tomb is on the sprawling grounds of Behesht-e-Zahra Cemetery, several miles south of Tehran on the way to Qom. We travel past the oversize hands holding a red tulip aloft, past the fountain of blood (water dyed red), which is mercifully silent. The bus turns off into a gigantic parking lot and pulls to a stop. We climb out and join the straggling crowd moving toward the shrine.

The smell of grilled meat wafts on the air, floating from a nearby concession stand. A few rosebushes are dwarfed by a sea of concrete. Revolutionary chants flow from a loud speaker. Elham looks around her with distaste, both of us thinking of the simplicity of Jamaran. "If he were here, I don't think he'd care for all this formality," she says. "Maybe the people think it's their duty."

Our bags are searched before we go in; Khomeini's tomb is a prime target for bombings of the sort that claimed the lives of hundreds of government leaders in the 1980s, when the Mujahedeen were most active in their battle against the mullahs. Vast marble floors alternate with carpeted spaces under a ceiling that reminds me of a warehouse. The tomb lies at the center, marble covered by a green cloth—the color associated with Islam. It is surrounded by a metal grille. The marble slab is a foot and a half deep in crumpled bills. A woman folds another bill and thrusts it through the grillework as I watch, pressing her lips against the metal and murmuring a prayer.

Elham searches out a prayer rug while I go about my interviews. I approach a family; the parents sitting next to their young son while a baby sister crawls on the smooth floor. They watch her play, seemingly in no hurry. The man says the usual things about Khomeini—how he delivered Iran from the corrupt moral influence of the West and renewed Islam. His tanned face is calm, his eyes surrounded by laugh lines. He speaks with quiet sincerity. "When we made the revolution, I believed Iran to be in truth diseased," he says. "I went to war to save my country, to save my honor."

His son was born while he was a prisoner of war, he tells me. "How old was he when you saw him for the first time?" I ask. His poise wavers. "Ten," he says. I look at the boy, who listens quietly, at his mother, who has the face of a woman schooled to patience. "Was it worth it?" I ask her. She hesitates, searching for the right words. "Yes, it was worth it," she says in a shy, soft voice. "It was for God. To please God, anything a man can do is still too little."

I repeat my question to the boy. He pauses for a long time, leaning against his mother's knee, and I wonder if he is too shy to answer.

Then he says: "My uncle was martyred in '61." That would have been 1982, in the early years of the war. His parents look sad, remembering. "If my *baba* had been martyred too, it wouldn't have been worth it," the boy says. He speaks with a touch of defiance, sudden tears in his eyes. He is twelve years old and has only known a father for the past two years of his life. "No, it wouldn't have been worth it."

His parents look away, their eyes damp. We share the silence. After a moment, I thank them and leave.

A few minutes later, I am interviewing a teenage boy who is memorizing verses for a Koran recitation contest. A grizzled man in army fatigues, walkie-talkie in hand, marches up to me. "You!" he barks, using the familiar form of speech in an unconscious—or deliberate?—act of rudeness. "Go over there. This is the men's section."

"I'm just asking some questions," I say. I show him my letter of authorization. He insists on escorting me to the women's section nonetheless, scowling the whole way. Elham comes up as he leaves, and I tell her what's happened. "What a jerk," I say. "He was so rude."

Elham is clearly disturbed. "Let's go talk to him," she says firmly. I follow in her wake, intrigued. She goes up to the man and engages his attention with a polite greeting. "It's a good thing that this lady is Iranian," Elham tells him. "I would suggest that next time you be a little more congenial. It would be nice to say a greeting. I think it would be better for Islam and Iran." The man refuses to look at her, though her black *chador* keeps him silent. "*Insha'allah* in the future it will be so," she says.

As we leave, I feel a wave of sympathy for my old friend. Not because the girl I knew has been reincarnated as a dogged woman, whose most cherished possession is a sample of the earth from Khomeini's grave, collected from as close as possible to the actual tomb. Not because her choices have turned her into an outcast among her family and friends. But because she struggles to maintain her ideals in a cynical world.

That, at least, we still have in common.

CONVERSATION at the home of an Iranian intellectual:

Mr. A., a lit cigarette held between thin brown fingers: "The revolution was undoubtedly a Western conspiracy." He takes a pull, the smoke wreathing around his silvery head. "It was ordered. Ordered by Amrika."

"Are you saying Khomeini was an American agent?" asks Mr. B.

Mr. A. shakes his head. "Khomeini did not serve any foreign power. But he was a tool that they were able to put in place and take advantage of, because they knew what he would do."

"He was an unconscious tool," Mr. B. says, nodding.

Our hostess serves tea and a chocolate cake baked by her daughter. The conversation whirls and eddies, but returns always to the iniquities of the Islamic regime: so-and-so's property seized illegally, a brilliant student kicked out of school on the grounds that she was not sufficiently Islamic, another student reprimanded for walking in a way that was deemed suggestive. "I was dressed in black from head to toe, but they said you sway your hips when you walk!" she tells me. Her striking face is tastefully made up, her hair pulled back in a sleek chignon. "Can you believe it?"

"The way I look at it is that this country is under occupation," says Mr. B., a young man with piercing eyes and a mustache. "This is how I explain it to myself."

"I wish the army of occupation was a foreign one," our hostess says bitterly. "They wouldn't hound people so."

"Is there anything positive about this regime?" I ask them. They think for a moment.

"There was a lot of loose living in the country before," Mr. A. concedes. "That's been severely curtailed."

"People are much more informed now," his daughter adds. "Social pressure has functioned to a degree as a lever, awakening people."

"The level of education in the schools is greatly improved," her mother says. "It's only in teaching history that they censor the truth. . . . And the bookstores are so crowded you can barely get in. This really delights me."

Mr. B.: "The people want to understand why they're so miserable."

Mashad
December 5, 1992

G HAMAR glides into the kitchen and sees me there, sitting at the table with my bread and cheese. Her *chador* is anchored miraculously on the back of her head, and her doleful brown eyes look just to my left as she asks, "Would you like milk?"

"No thank you, Ghamar."

"Because we have milk."

"No thank you, I'm having tea."

"It's no trouble, because we have milk."

"No thank you, I don't usually drink milk."

She asks me this every morning.

LATER in the day, Afzal and Ramin and I are returning from the produce store, a fragrant bundle of herbs tucked under Afzal's arm. The sky is white and overcast, the gold-brown leaves of the trees still dripping from last night's rain. Our breath puffs out in white clouds as we walk. On the way home we see an old man in an orange uniform, hefting cans of garbage. "Baba, isn't that Ahmad-Agha?" Ramin asks Afzal. Ahmad-Agha has been the neighborhood streetsweeper for twenty years.

Afzal calls out to him. The tall old man strides toward us stiffly, his joints no doubt aching in the damp chill. He embraces Afzal and they kiss on both cheeks, Ahmad Agha careful to keep his thick, muddy fingers from touching Afzal's coat. The old man's hands are spotted from some skin ailment, like his huge, leathery face with the outthrust lower lip. His head in its wool cap is swathed in white gauze for additional protection from the cold. "Where have you been, Ahmad-Agha?" Afzal asks.

"I've been around," the old man answers. "Where are you?"

"I'm in the same old place."

"I thought you'd moved away."

"No," Afzal answers. "Come visit us, have some tea with us." They say good-bye. As we walk on through the muddy streets, Afzal says, "When Ahmad-Agha was done with his work, he would come and sit on our steps. One day I asked him why. 'To keep you safe,' he told me."

This story reminds Afzal of another. It was twenty years ago, and he and some American friends embarked on a long hike across the mountains. They got lost, climbing one peak only to find another. By the time they heard the jingling of bells, they had run out of food. A herd of sheep appeared, followed by the shepherd. In his cloth bundle he had bread and yogurt.

The friends thought it the best food they had ever tasted. Afzal handed the old man a hundred tomans—several months' pay in those days.

The shepherd refused. His good deed had earned him *savab*, a blessing in God's eyes. "I won't sell the blessing," he told Afzal.

The Abbassi Hotel
Isfahan
December 14, 1992

THE cool wind blows through the open door to the balcony. Neil stands there under the blue sky, mild even in December, gazing out over the giant courtyard of the former Shah Abbas Hotel. Green grass, rosebushes, and white stone walkways are framed by the graceful arches so popular in Islamic architecture. The hotel is deserted, badly in need of a facelift and plastered with warnings against *badhejabi*—adequate covering is required for all women age nine and up. We seem to be the only guests. The maids and stewards haunt our footsteps, hoping for a tip, then return to some corner to sit idle. But the lofty, gilt-edged ceilings, jewel-toned tiles, Persian minia-tures, and stained glass still convey an air of sumptuous grandeur.

The man who took us on a private tour earlier today proudly showed off the suite that Anthony Quinn used during the filming of *Caravan* and the villa where Amir Abbas Hoveyda, the Shah's longtime prime minister (executed after the revolu-tion), shared his bed with his books. He took us next to the Shah's own suite, where the drapes were drawn and gloom shrouded the imposing four-poster bed with its avocado-green spread, now frayed and faded. In the dining room, the curva-ceous Iranian beauties depicted in the vivid mural on one wall have chalky gouges where their eyes were. Like Hoveyda, they were a casualty of the revolution. Our guide tells us they were defaced by the mother of a martyr. She considered this display of feminine sensuality an affront to her dead son.

When we return to our room, we find sitting on the bedside table a bowl of fruit and a plate of *gaz*, the nougat candy Isfahan is famous for. I call the front desk to find out who sent them. The once-surly manager is eager to inform me that the fruit and sweets come compliments of the Abbassi. "You should have told us you were guests of Mr. K.," he says reproachfully. I murmur something polite and hang up. His boss is a family friend. When we arrived, he was able to vouch that Neil and I were indeed married so that we did not have to produce the marriage certificate we carry with us.

I lie back on the bed, gazing lethargically at the rectangle of blue sky framed by the french doors. Neil comes inside and stretches out beside me. He is delighted that we are on our own for three whole days. This is my husband's first trip to Iran, and he has already learned that solitude is rare in this country, where social obligations rule supreme. But he senses my distance, my depression.

For two months we have been apart. For two months I have been on my own in Iran. The night-time telephone conversations with Neil often seemed to be my lifeline to sanity; he was the only person I could pour my heart out to as I experienced the hardships and wonders of living in Iran. I told him about playing tennis at the former Hilton Hotel—now the Independence. I played with their pro, who insisted I wear my *roupoush* as well as my scarf to avoid trouble with the authorities. How exhilarating it was to scramble around those red clay courts with the snow-capped Alburz Mountains in the distance. How odd to hear the thwack of tennis balls against the backdrop of the noon call to prayer. My scarf kept slipping off my head, making it impossible to play properly. Another day I decided to go swimming at their spa, but I backed out quickly with an excuse after I saw the murky water and slimy tiles. "I remember the Hilton when I was a child, it was the Royal Hilton then, and it was so fancy," I told Neil wistfully.

I told him about my interview with Zahra Mustafavi, Ayatollah Khomeini's daughter, and how she described her father as a man who insisted on self-reliance—in women as well as men. She told me she loved his sense of humor (though she herself was as outwardly dour as her father). She gave me a ride home in a shiny Mercedes, the driver negotiating the heavy Tehran traffic while she sat in the back, discussing plans for a forthcoming conference with an assistant.

I told him about my reunion with my Iran-Suisse classmates, a lively, intelligent group of women who'd just celebrated their thirtieth birthdays together. In an uptown highrise apartment, we talked over homemade wine and pizza, blue and feta cheese. I told him that some were single, some married or divorced; half of them worked, half were house-

wives, and all of them were disgusted with Islamic rule. And
how sitting in the back of the ancient cab that drove me to a
party in the nearby town of Karaj afterward, staring into the
hazy sunset, I thought, "I could live here. I could be Iranian
again."

Over the phone I couldn't stop talking to Neil. Now that we
are together again I can't start. I feel numb. He seems alien to
me. The life I've lived for the past two months, this Iranian
life, has fused into a hard shell that encases the person he
knows; the American Gelareh. I want to connect with Neil.
But to do so seems to threaten my forgotten self, the part of me
that is slowly unfurling in this lonely sojourn.

Neil does not know how to help me. But he stays beside me.
Eventually, I cry. The tears wash away the wall between us. I
allow myself to be American once again, no matter the risk.

OUR guide picks us up in one of the nondescript, aging auto-
mobiles that fill the roads of Iran, prepared to show us around
the city of Shah Abbas. Abbas was the sixteenth-century mon-
arch who put Isfahan on the map, building the rectangular
mall, the *meydan*, where the king and his courtiers played
polo, erecting the two gorgeous mosques, the royal palace, and
the vaulted bazaar that surround the *meydan* in graceful sym-
metry. The mall, known for centuries as Shah Square, became
Imam Square after the revolution. The Shah Mosque became
the Imam Mosque. But Isfahan's fame lies in the bridges and
mosques and palaces of Shah Abbas's reign.

Our guide turns out to be Jewish, one of the two thousand
remaining of what was once a thriving Jewish community.
Now, Greater Isfahan's four million–plus population numbers
more Christians than Jews. There are ten thousand Armeni-
ans here, he tells us, descendants of those who fled the Turkish massacres.

Numbers flow easily from our guide's lips and he showers us with historical detail, but he is deeply reticent otherwise. His eyes are shuttered, and he carries his tall, thin body with a stoop. Hunched over the steering wheel as he drives through a busy street on this cloudy day, he pulls to a stop suddenly, leaning across the passenger seat to open the door. He calls a greeting to a bent old man and beckons. The old man climbs in, bringing the smell of rain and rose water with him.

"*Salaam, haji,*" our guide says to the old man. The new-comer returns the greeting, resting against the seat with a sigh, then asks, "How is your *agha*?"

"My father passed on," our guide says, his eyes on the traffic.

"God rest his soul," the old man says. "It's the way of humankind."

"He's at rest now," our guide responds. "He suffered much."

He drops his friend off at the corner, near the Imam Mosque. The old man waves, walking slowly across the busy sidewalk, where men on stools sit before their typewriters, ready to write letters for the illiterate for a fee. Driving away, our guide becomes positively talkative. "When I was a boy, a playmate stabbed me in the side with a quilting needle because I was a Jew," he says. "That old man came to my rescue. He took me in until my parents came. He owns an *attari* shop on the corner." *Attars* sell herbs, potions, and perfumes.

"He's a Muslim?" I ask.

"Yes," our guide says. "He's a good man."

Later, as we are wandering through the deserted, tree-shaded grounds of Chehel Sotoon palace, he tells us his children are in America. "There is nothing for them here," he says. The call to prayer builds mournfully in the air. He has been telling us scraps of history to go along with the murals on the walls of the seventeenth-century mansion, murals depicting battle scenes, Nader Shah's conquest of Delhi, and the royal delegations that visited when Iran was a dwindling empire and Isfahan its capital.

Chehel Sotoon means "Forty Columns." We have come to the long rectangular pool that reflects and doubles the mansion's twenty columns, giving it the name. Our guide takes pictures of Neil and me standing there. I offer to take a letter for him to America and ask him to pose for a picture. I promise to send the photo with his letter, a letter from Isfahan by way of Silver Spring, Maryland. He almost smiles.

He takes his place in front of the palace, standing very still as if to occupy a minimum of space. Water pours from a sculpted lion's head into the pool, creating circles that spread ever outward. Water falls from the sky onto his face.

He looks into the camera as if he is looking into his children's eyes.

WE HIKE up a rocky bluff topped by a cylindrical wall made of mud bricks. This, our guide tells us, is a fire temple. Fifteen centuries ago, the ancient Persians came here to leave their dead in the Tower of Silence for the birds to pick clean. This was two hundred years before the Arab invasion that brought Islam to Iran. Iranians were Zoroastrians back then, worshipers of fire.

If the left eye went first, the soul was bound for hell, our guide tells us. The right eye, heaven. The mud brick enclosure has wide openings on each side so that the soul, once freed of the body, can take flight. Neil wanders over to one, looking down at the trees that line the road back to town. Our guide wanders off. I stand there in the middle of the silence, feeling the sweep of the wind.

A few moments later, Neil and I are making our careful way back down the rocky path. I am talking the whole time and turn around to make a point to Neil, just above me on the mountainside. I stop in midsentence. Before me, in a shallow depression, hides a couple. Fully clothed, they are locked in a passionate and clearly sexual embrace. Neil reaches me and looks to see what I'm staring at. Our eyes meet. "Well," says Neil with a straight face, "she's wearing complete *hejab*."

We hurry on down the hillside, trying to muffle our laughter. The couple never looks up.

A FRIEND takes us to the airport. As we drive through the city we are telling him how beautiful we found it. He agrees without enthusiasm. A moment later, he tells us there has been a stoning in Isfahan.

"When?" I ask, shocked.

"It was a couple of months ago," he says grimly. "A woman slept with her sister's husband."

The woman, he tells us, lacked the usual mitigating circumstances—a husband who was absent for long periods of time or unable to perform sexually. Our friend looks straight ahead as he tells the story, the blue sky bright behind him as the wind blows through the car. "It's what the *fatwa* decrees," he says, referring to the religious decrees issued by top clergy, which are binding as law.

Conversation ceases. I feel sickened. It is not only the savagery of what happened here that disturbs me, for one has only to read the newspaper each day—in the United States or any other country—to know that savagery is commonplace throughout the world. What disturbs me is that I see this stoning as part of the broader fabric of Iranian society. It exists on a continuum that begins with the demonization of the female form. This is a country where some orthodox families hide women's shoes as soon as guests take them off to enter a house —because the shoes are too evocative of the female body.

I look out the window, thinking of the couple embracing on the hillside.

December 17, 1992
Isfahan Airport

S IGN in the women's security checkpoint:

Badhejabi:

Hair that is excessively revealed in a provocative and repugnant manner

Clothing that reveals the body's curves in a provocative and repugnant manner

Makeup on the face such as lipstick or eyeshadow displayed in a provocative and repugnant manner . . .

Persepolis
December 18, 1992

I S YOUR husband Italian?" asks the man who has offered to guide us through the ruins at Persepolis, seat of the Achamaenid dynasty until it was burned down by Alexander the Great in 332 B.C.

"No," I say reluctantly. "He's American."

The man's face lights up, and he turns to Neil. "Thank you!" he says in English, bowing fervently twice. "Thank you."

Pasargad
December 18, 1992

H E'S AMERICAN? Really?" The man with the empty sleeve is questioning our driver. The driver nods, fingering his worry beads. We stand on a hilltop overlooking the grave of Iran's first great emperor, Cyrus—called Kourosh in Iran—who founded the Persian Empire in the fifth century B.C. Kourosh's domain encompassed what is now Iraq, Syria,

Jordan and parts of Afghanistan, Pakistan, the Soviet republics, and Egypt.

The man, a chance-met stranger who shares the vast, empty plain with us, turns narrowed hazel eyes onto Neil, smiles, and nods. "Amrika good," he says in English. Neil smiles back, saying something friendly in return. This man used to work as a guide to the antiquities during the time of the Shah, he tells me. The Americans always gave big tips, he remembers. Back then, he owned a pair of American binoculars that he used while hunting. He lost his arm on one of these hunting trips and was snakebit too. He tells me this in passing as he speaks with longing of those binoculars: "You looked through them, it was like whatever you were looking at was right there." He slants an assessing glance at me, and his voice takes on a wheedling tone. "If you bring me another pair, I will pay you. I'll give you a carpet in exchange. You should see the carpets they weave in my village."

I look at him with incredulity, amazed at the naiveté that coexists with the canny shrewdness in his eyes. I try to point out the impracticalities of his scheme; he listens with half an ear, hunkered down on that hilltop, his weatherbeaten face lifted to the breeze. It's clear to him that he's not getting his binoculars from me. He gives up, his cheerful ebullience undiminished, throws a bundle of assorted belongings over his shoulder and sets off with a wave.

I watch him lope across Kourosh's plain, heading for the patch of green that is his village. In the distance, the snowcapped mountains are dappled with sun and cloud. When we set out this morning from Shiraz, we drove through thick, ghostly fog, and the cold wind whistled through a hole in the side of the car. But now the sky is blue. The breeze tugs at the lone figure in the distance, his brown polyester pants flapping.

He won't ever own another pair of American binoculars, but to me he seems light and free.

Tehran
December 1992

I N THE bookstores that abound near Tehran University, I find, translated into Farsi:

- *The Joke*, by Milan Kundera
- *The Power of Positive Thinking*, by Norman Vincent Peale
- *Gone With the Wind*, by Margaret Mitchell
- *When Am I Going to Be Happy*, by Penelope Rusicenoff, Ph.D.

Tehran
December 1992

K IIANOM Asayesh, can you step in here for a moment, please?" I follow the government worker who has been guiding me through some official business and find myself in an alcove off the stairwell in this nondescript building in downtown Tehran. Neil joins us. I look at the man questioningly.

"Khanom Asayesh, I need a loan. Two hundred dollars."

I stare at him. My mind doesn't seem to be processing his request properly, but maybe it is, because I'm thinking, "I can't afford to lose this guy's cooperation."

"We'd be glad to help in any way we can, of course," I say automatically. I turn to Neil and say in English, "How much cash do you have? Give it to me."

I hand over fifty dollars. "I'm afraid this is all we have right now."

The man laughs nervously. "You're probably glad you don't have any more on you," he says, tucking the money away. "Thank you. Thank you very much."

"It was nothing," I respond by rote, turning away from him. I can't stand to look at him just now.

"It's these government workers, they don't get paid enough to make a living, poor souls," Khaleh Farah says later, over the phone. I can tell from her voice that she is distressed that I have seen this side of Iran.

But I can't forgive the shattering of my illusions. "I don't care," I answer. "It's still wrong."

Tehran
December 30, 1992

"THERE was this man I knew," our cabriver says reminiscently as he negotiates the downtown traffic. "He said to me once, 'How can I say "Death to Amrika"?

" 'I have a refrigerator, it's been working for fourteen years. It gives me ice from morning until night. How can I say "Death to Amrika?"' "

Mehrabad International Airport
December 31st, 1992

I BUY an aluminum juice pack from the snack bar—a Sundis brand, apple-lemon flavor—and walk back to the gate area. I sink down in the molded plastic chair next to Neil, heaving a sigh of weariness and relief. The lengthy good-byes, passport control, the ordeal of customs, the body search at security—all are behind us now. In a little while we will board the KLM jet and enter the familiar, reliable world of the West. I'll be able to take this scarf off my head, make phone calls that go through on the first try, buy plane tickets over the phone with a credit card, sleep in my own bed in my own house. I long for that bed, for the comfort of my American life bought at the price of the heartache I feel tonight.

The fluorescent lights hurt my eyes. Neil sits next to me as he has on so many occasions in so many airports, a pack of gum in his pocket and a book in his lap. It's hard to believe that only last year I despaired of ever winning permission for my American husband to visit Iran.

I drink my juice. It is cloying but cold. Neil looks up from his reading. "Do you realize it's New Year's Eve?" he says.

We look around us at the walls decorated with pictures of mullahs. At the bored revolutionary guard lolling next to a door. At our fellow passengers in their somber suits and *manteaux.*

"Do you think they'll give us champagne on the plane?" I ask.

"Maybe."

I set aside my Sundis and sit back, closing my eyes against the glare.

VII · Fault Lines

Silver Spring, Maryland
1993

LIST of ideas for infusing more of my culture into the life I live in America:

- Read more Farsi (How about a Farsi book club?)
- Read the *Iran Times*.
- Create a Persian room in the house—all carpet and cushions.
- Write my family more often.
- Call them more often.

THE telephone rings with that distinctive tone, more like a horn than a bell. Someone picks up. The wires crackle.

"Khaleh Farah?"

"Gel-gelis!"

"*Salaam!* How are you?"

"Gel-gel-jan, we miss you. I was saying just the other day, 'I hope we haven't offended her in some way.'"

"Offended me? How could you possibly have offended me?"

"It's just been so long since we heard from you, not since you left . . ."

"I'm sorry. I'm sorry. It's just that I've been really busy . . ."

CONVERSATION with a stranger curious about my name:

"What?"

"Iranian," I repeat.

He looks blank.

"You know. Iran. Iraq."

"Ohhh. *Eye*-ran."

"Actually, it's Eee-ran," I say, as I have thousands of times before. "Like Italy. Italian versus Eye-talian."

"Oh."

CONVERSATION with my friend Deb on a visit to Sacramento:

"I'm so tired of it all." Weeping. "I'm so sick of my heritage." Angry. "I wish I were completely vanilla. I wish I'd been born somewhere in the Midwest."

Deb, who was born in Nebraska, hands me more tissues, smooths my hair, pulls the blanket up over me.

"You need a rest," she says, her voice gentle.

CONVERSATION with Neil:

"You have to learn Farsi. It can't just be one of those empty promises. We have to make it happen. It's like this fault line in our marriage, that I can't share my whole world with you."

He looks at me sitting there with the box of tissues, several already wadded on the floor. We're up in the attic, where I now work. He's just gotten home from the office, still in suit and tie. His face is grave as he listens to me.

"Are we together on this? Are we?"

He nods at last. I search his face, wanting to be sure. His eyes meet mine steadily. He looks both serene and stern, he looks wholly committed.

I can breathe again.

CONVERSATION with a friend in Toronto, whose parents live in Iran:

"You're going to Iran again?"

"Yeah, I try to go every year."

"I went to Iran one time but I didn't like it. I didn't have a good time."

St. Petersburg, Florida
April 1994

CONVERSATION with a baby:
"Let's change your diaper," I tell my new daughter, laying her on the changing table. "I feel like such an idiot speaking Farsi to you. It feels so awkward. Who am I kidding? You can't understand."

Her eyes, bright and dark, hold my face. I stroke the hair off her forehead, my fingers arrowing across her scalp—a touch she has loved since birth. She drinks me in, my voice, my smell.

And I keep talking to her, in the grocery store, in the car, at our mommy group when all the other mothers are cooing to their babies in English.

She becomes my wordless confidante. Before long, I find it inconceivable that I would speak anything but Farsi to my child.

VIII · Crisis

Tehran
November 27, 1994

THE sky is gloaming when we wake. Last night, Mina's
first in Iran, she screamed and cried, keeping our hosts up
for hours. She is nine months old, too young to handle jet lag
with grace. We dress quickly and decide to go for a walk. After
sleeping the day away, it is a relief to trade our tangled bed-
clothes and scattered belongings for the cold night air.

We walk down the hill to Niavaran Park, the baby bundled
up in the stroller. The sound of city traffic grows as we leave
the quiet residential streets; the park is surrounded by busy
thoroughfares. The royal palace of the same name is nearby,
long since converted to a museum. But Niavaran Park is unchanged, still beautiful and well tended. Bright lights illuminate the avenues; the trees cast looming shadows.

Our path leads us to a glass hut where a silent young man
sits under a lumpy orange canopy—huge bags of cheese puffs

suspended from the ceiling. He sells us stale cakes in cello-
phane packages and tea bags in Styrofoam cups of hot water.
The transaction closes with *ta'arof*—the elaborate courtesy
ritual that is so quintessentially Iranian. I fall quickly into the
familiar pattern. Three times he says, "It is not worth it,"
when I attempt to pay. Three times I respond with "Please."
Eighteen tomans changes hands.

We sit on a stone ledge, cupping the steaming Styrofoam in
chilled hands. A late-night runner huffs around the perimeter
of a rectangular pool. The lit fountain is a rainbow of bright
spray, and the sounds of traffic are cushioned by the stillness
of the park. Caught up in the slow creep of uneasy thoughts, I
have little to say to Neil.

It has been two years since I last visited Iran. Now I am here
with my husband and new daughter. It is a momentous occasion, one I have dreamed of. But I feel no joy, none of the excitement and anticipation of prior trips. It is as if each trip has
peeled away layers of romance and novelty until at last I have
arrived at unadorned reality. And on this night, reality feels
bleak.

I came here seeking the sense of connection—to myself and
my past—that eludes me in America. But as I watch the light
play on the water and try to make sense of my jumbled emotions, my mind keeps returning to the image of the man in the
glass hut, alone in the dark spaces of the night.

ON THE way back, we have to keep the stroller on the street.
Iran's sidewalks are brief parentheses in the larger disorder of
water-filled gullies and stone slabs, tree roots and asphalt, all
jumbled together.

In my near-constant attempt to define my country and its
unique appeal, I find this disorder poignant. There is an elusive
quality that sets Iran apart from the gleaming, efficient West
in ways both repellent and appealing. It is the essence of the

Third World, of richness of culture and poverty of resources, of deprivation and burgeoning growth. It is depressing yet exciting, the unruliness bordering on chaos that prevails here. Everything in America seems restrained in comparison—the land has been tamed by concrete and the people by laws similarly impervious and uniform. I live in America in a well-ordered society—although a violent one—and thrive in its orderliness. Iran is not very violent; murders here retain intense shock value. But it is untamed. Life seems more accessible, less closed off.

Most Westerners see Iran as primitive and backward. Perhaps that is true, although the truth depends on one's viewpoint. Tales of Jeffrey Dahmers and Ted Bundys, of schoolyard massacres and drive-by shootings, are as shocking to Iranians as stonings are to Americans—and far more common.

I think of Iran as primitive in a different sense, in the sense of being closer to God, man, and nature. Here in Iran, everything is broken pavement, weeds growing in an atmosphere of infinite risk and possibility. Faith and myth are part of the fabric of daily living. Simple people stop in their tracks to pray when the *muazzin*'s call to prayer drifts from the mosques. Sophisticated people believe in miracles. ("Have you heard of the Blind Shaykh?" a beautifully coiffed relative asks a country acquaintance over tea one afternoon. "I hear he can divine where stolen jewelry is hidden.")

Such innocence is rare in the country where I make my home. I must bring my daughter halfway across the world to experience it.

My family here complains that Iranians become colder and more self-centered day by day, as the economy crumbles and the battle for survival worsens. Yet the fruit is ripe, the wash dries on the line, and when a car breaks down in crowded Tehran, there is no shortage of people stopping to offer advice, water, a ride.

Despite a web of taboos and conventions, lives are lived ad hoc, not ordered and groomed and managed. Mrs. Z., who sews, falls in love with the cloth seller and threatens to leave her husband and children. A great to-do ensues, many tears are shed, but all is soon smoothed over. She thinks better of her folly and goes home. Her brothers beat up the cloth seller. Her husband's family hushes up the rumors. Mr. Z. visits me in a Tehran living room less than a year later, with no hint of what has happened other than many more gray hairs.

Life goes on—no counseling, no divorce. A river overflowed its bounds, then subsided in the fullness of time to its own ordinary bed.

Tehran
November 1994

TIME goes by in a blur of disturbed nights and cluttered days. We seem to spend most of our time taking care of Mina. First-time parents, we panic when she develops a rash, rush her to the doctor, disinfect her bathtub every night. In between family gatherings I am busy arranging interviews for Neil, who will be writing a newspaper series on Iran at the end of this trip. There are no leisurely shopping expeditions, no trips to the museum. There are not enough hours in the day. Even so, I decide, four years after first returning to Iran, that it is time to visit the home of my childhood.

It is a few days before we leave Tehran for Mashad. We are at a lunch date downtown, meeting the man I have known since birth by the name Amoo—uncle. He married and later was divorced from my father's sister, my *ammeh*. He takes Neil and me, baby in tow, to a restaurant tucked away in a neglected garden. Over chicken kabab, we talk of family and the country's economic problems. Then we climb into Amoo's Mercedes, which only recently replaced the Volvo I rode in as a child. We are headed for Shemiran, the uptown suburb where I grew up.

Driving through the narrow streets, I am afflicted with double vision. I look at a hillside and see it twice—once as it is on this mild, sunny December day in the year 1994, once covered with snow in a year I cannot name. I see my father panting with exertion as he tries to change a flat tire while I stamp my feet next to the car. At home, Homajoon and Afsaneh will be getting worried.

Where our house once stood on its hilltop, there is now a fancy apartment building with lacy white ironwork and a gleaming new door. Standing there, I imagine that I am visiting an alternate future; that the fancy apartment complex has never been built and our house is still there, marching down the steep hillside: two tiers of rooms descending to the pansy beds, the green lawn, and the willow trees, followed by the twenty-three steps to the garage below.

I imagine a young woman walking out to throw both halves of the garage door open, then backing her car out into the alleyway, getting out with the engine idling, locking the double doors again, and driving away.

She has lived all her life in Iran except for a brief sojourn in the United States as a child. She lived through the revolution and dresses up her obligatory *manteaux* with the most interesting scarves she can find. She grumbles about traffic and air pollution and the cost of living. She works downtown. She knows all the best pizza joints. She reads Iranian poetry. She is married and has children.

She is the woman I would be today if my parents had not made a momentous choice years ago. Now I am someone else, someone defined by otherness. I drink black coffee. I use too many swear words in English but know none in Farsi. The lexicon of my daily life includes words like Honda, play group, linguine with clam sauce. For years I thought it normal to build my life entirely around work.

Sometimes I wake up in the middle of the night, the words of my first language bursting into my mouth from some long-suppressed place. For days afterward, the English words feel like foreign objects on my tongue, metallic and cold, like the loose filling of a tooth. I walk around full of hidden despair until I manage once again to forget my childhood self.

My uncle smokes a cigarette. I pose for photographs under the sign that still says Shaghayegh Alley in blue. We leave.

Weeks later, Neil regrets that I did not include Mina in those pictures. It is not until I come across the photos one day at home in St. Petersburg that I realize the choice was deliberate. When I look at the images, there is nothing to distinguish the woman I have become from the one I might have been.

No Mina. No Neil.

There is only a young woman in a black *manteau* and colorful scarf, smiling at the camera with eyes narrowed against the sun.

Tehran
November 1994

W E RETURN to Niavaran Park for a rendezvous with Minoo and Marjan, childhood friends. Both women work during the day, so we meet at night. Marjan and her husband lead the way to an open-air café in the park. A handful of families gather there, huddled against the frigid air. Music drifts from a loudspeaker and strands of bright lights provide a touch of cheer. Minoo has brought her two daughters, and the girls clamor at once for a snack. "Neil, Gelareh, do you want anything?" Minoo asks in English. We ask for tea.

Neil and I stand shivering, Mina in her stroller. I wiggle my toes, which are going numb. I do not want to be here, I think miserably to myself. Starting to pack for Mashad earlier today, I wished I were packing to return to America. I longed for my house in St. Petersburg, for the sun shining on the pines outside my bedroom window, for my washer and dryer. Yet when I was in St. Petersburg I dreamed of Iran, of the houses I grew up in, the mountains, the sky. I feel trapped in a cycle of futile nostalgia.

Looking around, I am deeply conscious of the shiny stroller, the warm fleece cover-up that protects my daughter from the cold, the matching magenta parka. I look at a family standing nearby and notice the dark, bearded face of the husband, the cheap parka, coarsely woven sweaters and baggy pants of the children, the pretty, discontented face of the wife. I want to pull away from them and preserve myself, Neil, and Mina in an island of Western wealth and superiority. Mina's costly accouterments, my husband's clean-shaven face and neon anorak, my own pretty raincoat and Chanel scarf—this is what I want for myself. The Iranians around me seem alien and poor and primitive. The child I was, dressed like these children, is alien too. I want to deny her claim on me.

I am overcome by shame. I hate myself twice once out of the ingrained self-loathing that comes from years of being convinced of one's own inferiority, and once for the symptoms of that disease, my instinctive attempt to distance myself from my own kind.

Minoo has come back with the food and drink. I go through the motions of helping her, trying to smile.

Mashad
December 1994

CONVERSATION among three of my relatives, unaware of my presence, as they watch Mina play:

Cousin X: "From a racial standpoint, the child is her father's race, isn't she?"

Dr. Y: "Naturally. I've never seen an Iranian baby who was this quiet. Cry, cry all the time."

Mrs. X: "Our race has been ruined, don't you think? The Arabs, the Mongols . . . we've become polluted."

Myself, tearing into the room in a fury and snatching up my child: "How dare you? How dare you suggest that everything good in my child is because of her American half? How dare you talk about Iranians this way?"

A babel of horrified denials, a fierce argument, chaos.

Afterward, my aunt wants me to apologize to Dr. Y.

I refuse.

Gonabad
December 15, 1994

THE weather is so cold that my aunts nearly called off the trip. Mina has fallen asleep in the bus, and I zip her into her hooded cover-up to keep warm. My cousin Soodi holds her while I lug the portable crib into the courtyard and into the quiet avenue under the pomegranate trees, setting it up with efficient snaps of each rail. Dayi Morteza's two sons, Farzad and Farshad, and Vida's sons, Reza and Rasool, come to watch me. Vida, a year younger than I, is my aunt, the product of my grandfather's third marriage.

"This is from Amrika?" asks Rasool, six, admiring the portacrib.

"Of course it is," Farzad, ten, answers with disgust. "Iranians aren't smart enough to build anything like this."

"Nonsense!" I say sharply. "We have many fine things."

"Like what?" asks Farzad, his dark eyes contemptuous.

"What about Persian carpets?" I say. "People vie for them all over the world."

"Oh, carpets," he answers, hunching his shoulders and turning away with disgust. "Those are worthless." He walks away with his head hanging down, his hands in his pockets.

"Kings want those carpets!" I shout after him, outraged and heartsore. I want nothing so much as to take his polluted young mind in my hands and scrub it clean.

But I have to tend to my own mind first.

Mashad
December 1994

DON'T forget your *vozoo*," Khaleh Farah says.

I am hurrying across the living room to grab my coat and a veil for a late-night visit to the Haram, the shrine of Imam Reza. In a few days we will be heading to Tehran again. Relieved that I will not leave Mashad without paying my respects to the Imam—who should have been my first priority, not my last—Khaleh Farah is nonetheless prepared to make sure I do it right. "You have to make *vozoo* before you enter the Haram," she reminds me, referring to the ritual ablutions required for prayer and visits to holy ground.

Our eyes meet, hers full of apologetic determination, mine holding defiance and doubt. My uncertainty is wide and deep, encompassing all the questions of my spiritual life, not merely this one. I don't know what to do. This is a drawback of thinking for yourself, of picking and choosing what you believe rather than offering obedience along with your devotion: it leaves you struggling to decide the profound issues of the universe as you're running out the door.

My cousins Ali, Laleh, and Reza have come to escort Neil and me to the shrine. They stand waiting. Tradition and expedience win the day. With an exaggerated sigh, I roll my eyes and hurry into the bathroom to wash.

In my head the voice of instruction—my mother's, I suppose—recites its litany as my wet hand swishes across bare brown skin: "Your face, three times, from hairline to chin. Your arms, from elbow to fingertips. Your feet, from ankle to toetips." (This is the part I hate, taking my socks off in winter.) "The part of your hair, from the crown of your head to the forehead."

The Haram is on Tehran Avenue, a street that in summer reeks of raw sewage. The locals blame the smell on the pilgrims, the impoverished ones who camp out on the sidewalks and in the grassy roadway medians, washing their clothes in the dirty water of the gullies that line every street. But there is no smell now as we drive down the avenue, the gold dome and twin minarets shining ahead in the distance.

Once, the Haram was surrounded by rug and bead sellers and hawkers of religious paraphernalia. Now, a new road project girds the shrine in a web of concrete ribbons, complete with cloverleaf and underpass.

But inside, the shrine still belongs to the people—the pickpockets and pilgrims, the mullahs and the mendicants, the regulars and the once-a-year visitors. Some of Mashad's prominent citizens volunteer here, Khaleh Farah has told me. I imagine sober, well-heeled citizens, garbed in the blue uniform of the Haram janitors, walking the mirrored halls with plumed dust mops held aloft.

Inside the main courtyard, our shoes checked, we lift the heavy Persian carpet that keeps the cold out in winter and slip inside. A blaze of light shines from colored chandeliers, bouncing off the refracted mirror of the walls. I am surrounded by the press of unwashed bodies, the smell of sweat mingling with the scent of rose water, sprayed at regular intervals by the janitors. All around me, pilgrims pause to caress the carved wooden doors, to kiss the ornate golden fixtures, to press their foreheads against the lapis tiles inlaid with convoluted Arabic script. Every fragment of this place is holy to them; they embrace it like a child its mother. I marvel as always at the centuries of craftsmanship but cannot summon a similar reverence.

Laleh, in smiling recognition of my ineptitude with the veil, has been carrying Mina. But when we reach the women's section of the room, she hands me the baby and weaves her way to a corner bookcase, searching for one of the dog-eared prayer books stored there. I shift my daughter uncomfortably in my arms and make my way to the corner of the room. Leaning against the wall, I settle down to wait. All around me, women from all echelons of society come and go. Some are as pushy as New Yorkers on a subway as they fight for enough space on the marble floor to say their prayers. Their prayer stones, the *mohr*, are trampled in a way that would constitute gross disrespect in any other context. Women hunker down in groups, holding babies or people-watching as they crack melon seeds between their teeth. Women bend in prayer, their lips moving silently. Women sob out their laments, free to bare their souls without earning so much as a second glance.

When Laleh's prayers are done, we try briefly to approach Imam Reza's tomb, but the crowd is too thick even on this late evening. I hardly care. For me, the tomb is not what is most sacred in this shrine. It is the faith of the worshipers who lap at its walls like an unceasing ocean, their hands reaching toward their heart's desire. Their bodies form a dark wave of humanity; now and then, a child is tossed to the tumultuous surface and passed hand to hand so he may be blessed when his outstretched fingers reach the prize. Polished by a million caresses, the metal grillework of the tomb gleams bright as far as human hands can reach and is dull above.

In the past, the faith of my mother and my aunts has offered me a link to what I saw as holy in this place. I have often sat apart on the marble tiles, wrapping my *chador* close, listening to their prayers and their weeping. Afterward they would smile at me through their tears, wipe their nose, and breathe deeply, tired and at peace. I remember sitting in a taxicab next to Khaleh Mina after one such visit two years ago, when she was recovering from the breast cancer that she was sure would claim her life. She worried about her children, who still needed her. I had listened to her heart-wrenching sobs and held her, and now I marveled silently as she sat so still and quiet, her hands folded in her lap, and said in her composed little voice, "It was a good Haram."

But tonight there is no one to serve as my intermediary with God. There is only my child, resting confidently on my hip, secure in my embrace. I watch her take in the sights and sounds, her eyes as dazzled as mine when I first came here as a little girl.

Her confidence frightens me. I shift her weight awkwardly in my arms. It is a weight I have become accustomed to in the months since her birth, yet tonight I do not feel capable of bearing it with any grace.

St. Petersburg, Florida
January 1995

How was your trip?" friends and acquaintances ask me. "It was great!" I say with a big smile. I slip into my role of Sophisticated World Traveler and offer up an exotic anecdote, humorous and not too lengthy. For fellow parents I throw in a horror story about traveling with a baby.

I no longer try to describe where I've been. It is not possible to capture in a few sentences the essence of a journey, a pilgrimage that is of the mind and heart as well as of the body. I am learning that a pilgrimage is a private thing, not easily shared. There are places we go where the people we love cannot follow.

I fall into the pattern so familiar from past trips—the frenzy of actions intended to make my life more Iranian (a new Teflon pot, ideal for cooking rice for three; albums in which every picture from the trip is painstakingly labeled; new Iranian videos). And then the gradual relinquishing of an impossible burden. My grief is all the greater because I do not understand the feelings that surged darkly forth during this trip. I am steeped in a sense of guilt and failure. It is only when I pray that I come close to feeling at peace, allowing myself to believe, little by little, that I can trust the links that bind me to my country, my family, and my past.

Morning, noon and night I stand swathed in thin white cotton patterned in pale purple, my bare feet standing on the prayer rug that Khaleh Mina bought for me long ago. I use a *mohr* from Homajoon, a veil belonging to Khaleh Farah, a set of amber worry beads Neil and I bought in Shiraz. I say the Arabic words by rote, seeing in my mind's eye my mother and my aunts, my grandmothers and the women who came before them, my own childhood self—all murmuring and bending and rising in a rhythm that spans the centuries.

Often it feels meaningless, but I keep going anyway, for now.

Yesterday I noticed that my veil was taking on the scent of my skin, cool cloth imbued with the essence of my devotion.

IX · Connection

Mashad
September 18, 1995

STILL not married, Ali-jan?" Homajoon teases at our welcome feast. "Aghdas-jan, I thought you'd have found him
a wife by now." Ali's mother, sitting on the red Persian carpet
that covers Khaleh Farah's porch, laughs and thumbs her
worry beads. The night is cool but comfortable, all the porch
lights are on, and about twenty of us are sitting beneath the
starry sky while the younger members of the clan talk inside
the house. A running child knocks over my tea glass and Ghamar goes to get me another. Mina, glued wide-eyed to my side,
sits up alertly when she sees Giti-jan bringing the cake she
baked in our honor: yellow with cocoa icing and swirls of fresh
cream. "Cake!" she whispers urgently in my ear. "Not before
dinner," I answer. Then Giti-jan starts cutting into her confec-
tion and handing out plates, and I give in. "Okay. A small
piece."

Ali is laughing, used to being teased about his bachelor status. "Aghdas-jan was following this girl at the airport," he says with a sly glance at his mother.

"The airport," I groan. "Wonderful. They get married and someone asks, 'What do you have in common?' 'Well, we both like to travel.' You may as well ask the grocer to find him a wife, Aghdas-jan."

Everyone laughs, including Aghdas-jan.

After dinner, Khaleh Farah wants to schedule the Gonabad trip. I want to wait until Mina has recovered from all the traveling, but Khaleh Farah has other ideas: "I think we should go this week, while there are still grapes on the vine."

"You think there'll still be grapes on the vine by Thursday?" Ali asks, looking dubious.

"Let's find out," Khaleh Farah says, chuckling. "Let's send a team to examine the state of the grapes."

Mashad
September 20, 1995

I SIT on the bottom step leading down into Khaleh Farah's garden, watching Mina play. She stands naked at the garden's edge, trying to take the hose from Khaleh Farah. My aunt lets her have it and Mina aims it randomly, watching the clear water mingle with the dust on the flagstones. The sun catches the red tints in her brown hair. She turned eighteen months a couple of weeks ago.

Homajoon comes out on the porch, moving in the lazy way that seems particular to our visits to Iran. She shields her eyes against the glare of the afternoon sun with a hand and stares wistfully at the dusty leaves of the fig tree. Suddenly her gaze sharpens. "A ripe fig!" she cries. "See? Over there." Homajoon points, excited.

My mother was deeply disappointed to miss Khaleh Farah's figs, and Khaleh Farah is determined that her sister shall have this one. I take the old wooden ladder my aunt fetches from the corner of the courtyard, and set it against the sturdy trunk of the tree. I start to climb, complaining all the while about going to so much trouble for one fig.

The ladder slips and I shriek. The leaves shower me with fine dust as I part them with questing fingers. Finally, I find the right branch, pull it down, and Homajoon plucks the round fruit, dusky purple fading to green at the stem. She eats it slowly, offering pieces to us all. Mina watches in fascination, the water from the hose pouring onto the ground unheeded. Climbing down the ladder, I show her how the leaves of the plane trees, curled like arthritic fingers, crunch underfoot. Her laughter makes all of us smile.

A minute later Mina is crying because Khaleh Farah has turned off the water. "We can't waste water, you see," my aunt tells her. "A lot of people don't have water." Mina continues to hold on to the hose, crying. As a compromise, Khaleh Farah hauls out the red plastic washtub Ghamar uses to wash clothes. We fill it with water, and Mina steps in gingerly. The water slowly heats in the sun, and she squats down, sitting there "washing" the dusty clothes she shed when we came into the garden. She shares her tub with a rubber duck from home and an empty vitamin bottle.

Khaleh Farah disappears into the house. Soon we hear her voice calling from the basement, which has small windows opening onto the courtyard at ankle level. She calls me over and hands out a rolled piece of carpet. I unroll it in a shaded corner of the yard. My aunt bustles out with a blanket which she spreads out, tossing a pillow or two on top. Homajoon, her fig eaten, stretches out with a sigh. Khaleh Farah hikes up her green polyester dress and washes her bare feet in the water of the hose, then lies on her side next to Homajoon. Her short dark hair, flattened and spiky from her wimple, is uncovered in the privacy of the back yard. We rest in silence, soaking in the sunshine.

Afzal steps outside in his brisk way to hang a few clothes on the line that stretches the length of the porch. Mina's bib already hangs there, the yogurt from breakfast washed out. The doorbell rings, and soon Maryam wanders out to join us. Her class was canceled, she tells her mother, lying down on the blanket. "You forgot to lower the *hasir*," Khaleh Farah says idly, referring to the bamboo blinds used to keep the house cool in summer. "The black cat was able to get in. I saw its pawprints."

Maryam, dozing on her back with her arms crossed over her eyes, doesn't answer. I stay seated on the steps, my face lifted to the bright sky, my thoughts drifting lazily.

Maybe I'll plant a garden like this at home, I think to myself, and Mina and I will watch the sun go down as we water it.

Mashad
September 21

I saw a book that mentioned Mr. Asayesh," Afzal tells Homajoon at lunch.

"Mr. Asayesh?" I say, surprised. Baba is always referred to as Dr. Asayesh. They don't answer me, engaged in their own conversation. After a moment I realize they must be talking about Aghajan, Baba's father. How old was I when he died, I ask Homajoon.

She thinks back, one elbow propped on the table. "Aghajan was in prison when I was pregnant with you," she says. "Because we'd gone to see him and I remember they told me to wear a headscarf and a long-sleeved outfit. In the waiting room I got sick. He asked me, 'What's wrong?' Your *baba* told him, 'We're expecting our second child.' He went to prison one other time, when you were around the age Mina is now. He died soon after that."

"I barely remember him," I say.

"He loved you so much," Homajoon answers.

"Why?" I ask, longing for some specificity to bridge the gap between me and this man, who has never been more than a blurred face hovering on the edge of my memory.

"Because he said you were just like your *baba*."

Mashad
September 22, 1995

WHEN we come down for breakfast, Mina in my arms in her turquoise footed sleeper, rubbing her eyes drowsily, she asks where Havagova is. This is her best approximation of "Khaleh Farah" and "Khaleh Mina."

My aunts are delighted to be called Havagova. Khaleh Farah roots around in the basement for a dolly for Mina. Khaleh Mina, veiled in black from head to toe, takes her to the park, trailing after the little girl in the floppy white sun hat for two hours.

When Khaleh Farah prays, facing the sunlit window in the television room, Mina bends and straightens in imitation. Giti-jan, popping over from across the street for a chat, promises to make her a veil. It is soon complete, a pink flowered *chador* that Mina wears for all of one minute, wrapping it tightly around her head, the soft floral framing a face that is all sweet innocence. "How pretty!" we exclaim. Instantly, she tears the veil off and romps across the living room.

Afzal catches her there when he comes home for lunch, sitting on the floor in the middle of the big carpet, and kisses her so hard she falls over.

Later, Afzal pretends to make a phone call: "Hello? This is Havagova calling. Your servant."

HOMAJOON, who has promised to help me this trip in Neil's absence, has the chore of giving Mina a bath before bed. Khaleh Farah insists on joining her. Sitting on the green baize chair in the living room, I listen to the noises coming from behind the closed metal door to the *hammam*, where Mina is bathed in a washtub next to the shower and the new Western toilet. I hear the sisters gasp and coax and occasionally giggle. Mina starts to howl. I sip my tea, trying to decide whether to intervene. A clean toddler finally emerges, swathed in towels and cradled in her grandmother's arms.

"What happened?" I ask.

Mina herself answers, rubbing her eyes. "*Saboon!*" she says accusingly. Soap.

Homajoon and Khaleh Farah look guiltily at me, then at each other. They burst into laughter. "She gave us away, sister," Khaleh Farah says, wiping her eyes.

"We'll have to watch ourselves around her," Homajoon says. "She can tell on us now."

Gonabad
October 2, 1995

DAYI Morteza wants Mina to hold his hand as she negotiates the gravestones of the cemetery at Nowqab. She refuses, pulling her hand away and tucking it behind her back. She sees a low ledge that would be good to climb and heads that way, her red shirt and denim overalls a bright splash of color against the arid landscape.

"She wants to do everything herself," Morteza tells me, preparing to follow her. "She's just like you when you were that age." I make a face at him, used to hearing unflattering stories of my rebellious childhood. Gathering my veil around my waist, I walk over to the graves where my uncle and cousin lie, killed in an earthquake soon after we left for America.

While the rest of us pay our respects to the dead, Dayi Morteza shadows Mina. He is bent over double as he walks next to her, ready to catch her if she should fall.

Tehran
October 13, 1995

A LI, who has traveled from Mashad with Homajoon and me to see us off on the long trip home, takes Mina for an outing. It is our last day in Iran, predictably manic. I divide my time between packing four suitcases and greeting the visitors who come to Tooran's guest room to say good-bye. I am sick with a cold, hopelessly overwhelmed, and profoundly grateful to have Mina taken care of.

My cousin brings her back when it's dark. He has taken her to the park and bought her a bunch of the bananas that are so expensive here, along with a new ball. Mina rests contentedly in his arms, clutching both prizes. The ball is white with pale blue stripes.

"Do you think you could make room for it in your suitcase?" Ali asks diffidently.

"Of course," I answer.

"Mina-jan, don't you forget us," he says to her, placing her in my arms. His black eyes are glittering with tears. He turns away.

"She'll remember you every time she plays with it," I say, feeling deeply the inadequacy of my words.

X · In Between

St. Petersburg, Florida
July 16, 1997

THE doves start cooing with the dawn. The morning sun slants across the wooden floorboards, bringing the red hues of the Persian rug alive. A shaft of light captures Neil's tired face as he sits in the rocker, his hand encompassing the small body of our three-day-old son. Max, still rounded in a fetal curl, rests on his father's shoulder. He is dressed in the well-worn pink and turquoise sack Mina used as a baby. It fit her until a year ago, hanging down around her shins. Now it bunches up softly around our son's bent, scrawny legs, papery from the newness of their exposure to air.

A Band-Aid covers much of Max's right heel, from the PKU screening yesterday. Neil's hand pats and pats in an erratic rhythm. The light limns the lines of fatigue on the father's face, the curve of the baby's cheek, the downy head that bobs up and down as he snuffles and nuzzles and, eventually, burps.

On the cheap black stand next to the changing table, my mother has placed a vase with four pink roses—one for each member of my family. On my side of the bed, the bassinet holds a tumble of twisted blankets. In the closet, a plastic hospital bag overflows with freebies from the formula companies and the powder-blue tubing of the sitz bath. Outside our windows, the bunched green clusters of pines wave in the summer breeze, the pine needles glossy in the sunlight.

My eyes take it all in, and my exhausted mind recognizes some import to this moment. This is it, I think. This is life. For a moment it takes my breath away.

Then I turn over to go back to sleep, gratefully reaching for my pillow and unconsciousness. If it hadn't been for the light, I think as I drift off, the morning light pouring in the window, bathing all in glory, I would have seen only our daily toil. I would have missed the moment.

January 6, 1998

I AM terminally late with holiday cards. I wonder morosely if I have ever gotten them out on time. This year I was still working through my list of birth announcements when the holidays rolled around. Even though Max was born in July.

I finish the card I'm writing and go in search of a swatch of saffron to tuck into the envelope. This is a gift I like to give now and then, easily done since I bring so much of it back from each trip to Iran.

At the fridge I hunt through the egg compartment in the door, looking underneath the bulbs of garlic, behind the jar of powdered Omani lemons. Wedged in the corner I find what I'm looking for—a thick bundle of stamens, brittle as straw, tied in string and wrapped in cloudy plastic. The whole thing is about the size of two fingers. The stamens are gold at the tips, white at the roots, and deep orangey red in between.

I untie the string. It is a distinctively Iranian bit of string: cottony, thick, and white, unfinished-looking. Here and there it is stained yellow from the hands of whoever plucked these stamens from the flower. I hurry through the process of separating a bundle, eager to cross this task off my list. But my mind is far away, hosting an unbidden image. I see a mass of purple flowers spread out on a cloth in Khaleh Farah's living room, my aunt sitting on the carpet by the oil stove, working through the pile, joined intermittently by the visitors who come and go in her house. I see Khaleh Farah's worn, capable hands, the blunt fingers stained saffron yellow as she bundles the fresh stamens and fumbles with the piece of string, rooting in one of her kitchen drawers for the odds and ends of plastic. She tucks the bag in my hand as I climb up the steps to my room, packing to leave once again.

I retie the string carefully, fancying that my hands have touched hers today.

January 11, 1998

KHALEH Mina asked me today, once again, if I know what might have become of Mammad's book.

My cousin asked for this book over a year ago, during my last visit to Iran. It was one of a set of two and took me a long time to find, for the subject is an arcane computer software program used in city planning—Mammad's specialty as an engineer.

I have a special place in my heart for Mammad, whom I remember best as a busy, extroverted toddler running into our Tehran house in his turquoise terrycloth outfit, babbling cheerfully as he investigated the premises. Back then, he was oblivious of the tears that filled Khaleh Mina's eyes when she talked to my mother, their worried eyes following that bright streak of turquoise. "He has such good balance," I told Khaleh

Mina once. "That's a sign that his hearing can't be that bad."
But Mammad's hearing problems were congenital and permanent; and so were his brother Ali's when Khaleh Mina was delivered of her second child a year later.

At twenty-seven, Mammad is fully conscious of his handi-
cap and handles it with poise. He has a degree in engineering,
a talent for being the life of the party, and a wonderful sense of
humor. So when he asked me to find him these particular
books, I mentally filed his request at the top of the list gener-
ated by each trip to Iran (a picture of Madonna for Ali, a book
on Unidentified Flying Objects for Hameed, an exercise book
for Soodi, art supplies for Shadi . . .)

I bought the books. I sent them to Canada, where my parents were charged with assigning them to one of the numerous
friends traveling to Iran. Given the unpredictability of the Iranian postal service, this circuitous route is preferred for any
object of value.

Months have passed, and Khaleh Mina tells me that Mammad has still not received the second book (Thank you so
much for the first one).

I promise to try and track it down. As I hang up, I feel overcome by a familiar lethargy. When I ask my mother about the
book, she says helplessly, "I don't know what we did with
them. I think we sent them with Dr. Mahdavian. I'll check
around the apartment."

I ask my sister, whose recollection is equally hazy. My in-
quiries jog everyone's memory, and eventually we narrow the
possibilities to a friend of my uncle's wife, who delivered our
packets to Tooran's house in Tehran. Still pessimistic, I call
Khaleh Mina and tell her to check with Tooran.

I feel a disproportionate delight when the book surfaces in
Tooran's closet. Mammad's sister Soodi retrieves it on her
weekly trip to Tehran, where she is enrolled in university.

Mammad receives the book at last—eight months after I bought it, five months after it got to Iran, almost a year after he made the request.

The problem goes beyond the slow mails, the expensive telephone calls, or the faxes routed through the one relative who owns a machine. It is as if the futility of trying to bridge the distance between Iran and America creates a collective paralysis, which addles our judgment. It keeps us from making the handful of phone calls that would cut through the Gordian knots. Instead, words and objects are passed mouth to mouth and hand to hand until they get lost along the way.

I imagine the millions of molecules of air across the Atlantic Ocean compressed into a dense, viscous fog, a gray abyss that swallows everything—Mammad's book, our words and our love and our good intentions. The fog emits fumes of forgetfulness and torpor. It deadens the voice of our deeper self, the voice that speaks most clearly in the small hours of the morning, telegraphing into the darkness: I love you, I miss you, I want to tell you . . .

February 25, 1998

I COVER the computer, gather my things, and let myself out of the guest house. The main house seems quiet; the children must be napping. My feet trample rustling leaves and a soft carpet of pine needles as I walk to the weathered wooden gate that hangs, slightly crooked, in the fence surrounding the back yard. The metal latch falls back into place with a click. The soil is loamy beneath my feet as I enter the front yard. Oaks and pines mingle their branches above my head. The sea breeze carries the scent of orange blossoms. Late afternoon sunlight reflects in the rainwater pooling in the cupped surface of oak leaves scattered across the brick driveway.

The mellow light, the greenness, the wooden gate hanging over soft earth—all remind me of Gonabad. When I told Khaleh Farah the other day of our rainstorms, she told me they have had a lot of rain and snow in Mashad as well. She worries that the walls around Aghajoon's garden will tumble down at last.

My heart contracts when I think of this conversation. I push away my recollection of a time when I tried not only to save Gonabad but to make it new again. It was in 1995, before Dayi Morteza's death. I called a family meeting, and everyone pledged money for maintaining the property. But as soon as my plane left Iran, the status quo reclaimed my family. Khaleh Farah's sporadic and valiant efforts kept things going, but, for the most part, Gonabad was left to the sun and the wind, undisturbed by workmen or visitors.

Nowadays I no longer battle the immutables of space and time. I have let sadness into my heart, surrendering to the inevitability of Gonabad's decay. My grief is cushioned by acceptance.

Acceptance? Who am I kidding? I am cushioned only by distance and the fervent hope that the walls are still standing at winter's end, when Khaleh Farah will travel south again, doing what she can to hold back the tide.

I cross the driveway to my car, passing the sitter's car parked behind me. For a moment, I stop to gaze at the tumbled blue surface of the sea, barely visible through a row of bottlebrush trees bordering the grassy lot across the street.

The realization comes to me gently: I am not done with fighting to bridge the distance. But in this year of my son's birth, when the ocean and the whirlwind unfolding of my own life separate me from my family in Iran, I am taking a rest.

February 27, 1998

I FIND a letter from Nasrin tucked in the back of my 1990
journal. She writes that the rains are incessant in Rasht, that
the family hopes to move to Mashad soon—from the humid
verdant shores of the Caspian to the dry heat of the *kavir*. "The
children are fighting," Nasrin closes. "I need to go." I imagine
the two small boys home with Mother, and Father coming
home at the end of the day to take Farshad on his lap and help
Farzad with his homework. He did that for six years after Nasrin's letter was written—first in Rasht and then in Mashad—
until the day the driver of the tractor-trailer misjudged the distance as he passed a government car on the highway.

Dayi Morteza was in that car. The tail end of the rig struck
the very window he chose to rest his head against. He had told
the rest of the television crew, on their way home after an as-
signment, that he felt like a nap. Twenty minutes down the
road, in Mashad, Nasrin did not know she was now a widow.

My father reached me in London, where I waited with Mina
for the flight to Tehran. I lay in bed that night in my hotel room
dry-eyed and wakeful, Mina sleeping at my side, and wondered what to do with the shirt I had bought for my uncle,
striped in maroon and green and navy.

I turn over the envelope, studying the cheap, blue-veined
paper. On the front, four stamps depict a turbaned cleric. There
is a blue and red air mail sticker below. On the back, the tear I
made opening the letter separates the beginning of the send-
er's address from the end.

Morteza Ghassemi. Rasht. Morteza Ghassemi. Rasht.
Morteza Ghassemi.

When your name is said now your sisters get a pinched,
hopeless look on their faces. Your brother looks away until his
eyes are dry again.

How could this have happened? I couldn't be more confused if I had seen with my own eyes God waving the wand that made you, in an instant, disappear.

"Your place is empty," we would write each other across the years in too few letters—maybe five spanning two decades. But I always knew that your arms would be waiting to embrace me at the end of the too-long airplane ride. I always knew your address.

Your place is empty. And this time I don't know where to find you.

February 28, 1998

O UR FRIEND Paul was over today. He works at All Children's Hospital downtown but does home improvement projects on the side. I've drawn up a list for his consideration. I feel tense as I bring up the project that means the most to me: a wooden platform bed for the balcony between the children's room and ours. My thirty-sixth birthday is coming up in April. This is to be my present, a *takht* like the ones that sit under the trees in cafes and private homes in Iran, covered with a Persian carpet, the scene of meals and naps and conversations over the samovar.

I have no intention of trying to carry my samovar upstairs, but I harbor visions of starry nights with Neil and me and the children bundled up on a sleeping bag, and lazy afternoons of tea and gossip when my mother and sister visit. Khaleh Farah is even sending me the family *pasheh-band*, the square gauzy tent of mosquito netting that we slept in each summer in Gonabad.

I don't want to explain all this to Paul, so I give him the bare bones and try not to feel defensive when my requirements bring a perplexed look to his face. Neil tries to help explain the

concept, and we pace out the dimensions on the porch, Paul
plying his measuring tape. I carry Max on my hip, and Mina
dances out onto the balcony to see what everyone is up to.
Overhead, the pines sway in the sun and breeze. Below, the
back yard is saturated from an El Niño winter. I glance irrita-
bly at the clutter of plastic toys from the summer before last
and at the asparagus fern that has fallen from its tree perch
above and spills untidily out of a broken pot. Mina tries to look
through the porch railings, which are wide enough to allow a
four-year-old to fall, and I wave her back. Moments later she
returns the favor, yelling at the top of her voice in Farsi: "*Maman*, step back from the railings!"

I tell Paul I have a picture that may help him understand
what I have in mind, hand the baby to Neil, and take Mina
downstairs. The living room is dark on this cloudy, drippy Saturday. "No, I won't tell you a story about Dark Side," I say to
Mina, whose favorite television show these days is *Super-
friends*. "I have to find a picture in this book." I am leafing
through my volume of *Persia: Bridge of Turquoise*, a gorgeous
pictorial of Iran published in the time of the Shah. It takes me
fifteen minutes, but finally I find the photo I am looking for.

When the men come in from checking the rotting board-
walk in the back yard, I show Paul the picture. I wait warily for
the gleam of curiosity in his eyes, for the inane or insensitive
comment. Instead, Paul looks with interest at the image of an
old man and his wife sitting cross-legged on a *takht* in their
spacious yard, a samovar before them. The woman is holding
her white veil across her face with one hand while she pours
tea from a china teapot with the other. "I see," says Paul. "This
is"—I tense as he hesitates—"something to do with your
country."

"Yes," I say, relieved at the neutrality of his comment, the
lack of inquisitiveness.

Paul looks at the picture more closely. "That looks like cedar to me," he says. "I could . . ." and he goes into details of the technical possibilities. He draws me a rough sketch. I reject the idea of a pedestal base—I want the *takht* to have the traditional four legs. "I'm homesick, basically," I tell Paul, lowering my guard now that I feel reasonably certain he won't tell me any hostage jokes.

"I can see that," he says.

THAT night, I make *sabzi-polo* for dinner. I don't view this as real Iranian cooking, since the meat in the dish is imported Persian Gulf tuna out of a can. But Neil, whose appetite for Iranian cooking far outstrips the occasional rices and stews I dish up, is delighted. Both of us are eager to wrap up our elaborate bed and bath routine with the children so we can go downstairs for dinner. We kneel side by side next to the tub in the canary yellow bathroom, Neil soaping Max while I drizzle shampoo on Mina's head. She sloshes around wildly, soaking my leggings. "Settle down!" I yell. None of us is conscious of switching languages as we speak—Farsi when Mina or I address each other, English when Neil is involved in the conversation, although—thanks to years of sporadic lessons and three trips to Iran—he contributes the occasional comment in Farsi.

Nearly an hour later, the children are both in bed; Neil spending a few final moments with Mina. I kiss her goodnight and bend over the crib where Max sleeps for a final caress. On my way out of the darkened room, I glance at the bulletin board in the corner, which I filled three years ago with pictures from our 1995 trip to Iran. It was one of our happiest. I never replaced the photos with ones from our 1996 trip, the one we spent mourning Dayi Morteza. On the bulletin board, Homajoon looks out at me in pink lipstick and a dark gray veil sprinkled with tiny white flowers. She was standing in the town square in Gonabad when I took that picture. In another, Mina stands naked in a red plastic wash tub in Khaleh Farah's sunny back yard, the fig tree and purple asters in the background. The bottom row shows Mina asleep in my arms on the bus to Gonabad, Mina toddling along the avenue through the pomegranate trees, Mina with her nose pressed against a store window, Ramin at her side.

"Don't forget to put on Valjean," Mina says as I step out onto the landing. This is what she calls her current favorite tape, the musical *Les Miserables*.

After dinner I stand by the stove to finish getting the *tahdig* out of the Teflon pot I use for Iranian rice. This bottom layer of rice crisped in oil, yogurt, and saffron is a traditional favorite, but it is not easy to extract, even from a Teflon pot. As I hack away with a plastic spatula, squinting to protect my eyes from the stray kernels that fly with each stroke, I have a sudden mental image of my mother doing the same thing, her body braced, her face a study in grim determination.

Neil says, "We need to get the samovar cleaned up before your parents come. Put that on your list for Norooz."

I bought the samovar after my 1996 trip to Iran. I called up the Iranian grocery store I used to patronize in Rockville, Maryland, and ordered it—a steel urn from Germany with blue and white china handles and a steel teapot. It is electric, more practical than the old-fashioned kind with their wicks steeped in oil.

Buying the samovar was part of my familiar posttrip cycle of grief, despair, and determination. Like my other efforts at bringing the two halves of my life together, it eventually petered out, leaving a residue of hopelessness. My homecoming frenzies seemed to accomplish little more than to bridge my journey from grief to forgetfulness. Yet over time, the small things—the prayer rug I started using after the '94 trip, the bulletin board I put up in '95, the samovar in '96—have melded with the big things, like the Farsi class we started with a few like-minded families a year ago. Today, the strands that seemed so meaningless individually are wound together in a pattern that promises a kind of balance.

By the time I've finished with the *tahdig* and wiped the innumerable kernels of rice from the stove, the bishop of Digne is telling Jean Valjean, "I have bought your soul for God." I pass the dining table on my way to the laundry room and catch a glimpse of Xeroxed paper covered with my own tiny Farsi handwriting. The Norooz play. Mustn't forget to take that tomorrow, when we go to *Barname-ye-Kudak*. There are three families in our weekly Farsi program, and with the Iranian New Year coming up on March 20, we have decided to perform a short play. I adapted a favorite story from my childhood: "Flowers came, Spring came." A story of a wicked *Div* who won't let spring come to the desert. So the heroine, Nokhodi ("Little Pea"), does battle with the demon.

At the touch of her sword, the *Div* turns into smoke. Spring flowers bloom, transforming the wasteland.

March 15, 1998

IT IS Sunday, and after Neil returns from his weekly tennis game, it's my turn to leave the diaper bag behind. I wave good-bye with a giddy sense of freedom, heading for a nearby pancake house, where I spend a couple of hours with my journal and a novel. On the way home, I stop at Boston Market to pick up dinner. The restaurant's bright red trim and shining electric lights are a garish contrast to the softness of a sunset sky, clouds lit from within in shades of gold and pink and orange. Driving down Fourth Street in the gloaming, I suddenly see myself as if from above, my car moving across a living map. I travel through the flatness of St. Petersburg in the fading Florida sunset, and the image spreads to encompass the country around me, America, and then the planet; until on the other side, where it is not yet dawn, I can see Iran. All the connections are visible.

It is all a matter of perspective, of backing far enough away from the here and now. Most of the time I am embedded too deeply in my immediate experience. On those nights when my heart is full and memories surface, I have to convince myself that the moon gilding the pines outside my window is the same that will shine soon on the lantana bordering the sidewalk outside Khaleh Mina's house, on the fume-hazed, teeming streets of Tehran, on the still garden in Gonabad.

In the car, the smell of rotisserie chicken rises in waves from the overheated foil bag. A country music singer complains: *"Them politicians treat me like a MUSHroooom, they feed me bull and keep me in the blind."* The lights of the business district flash by—the ice cream parlor where Mina orders the unnatural blue and yellow ice cream called Superman, the restaurant where we can count on getting fed even after ten o'clock at night.

Like a rubber band released after a stretch, my breadth of perspective shrinks, snapping back into the here and now.

NIGHT has fallen. Driving alone through the darkness, my thoughts stream like ribbons in the breeze, fluttering out of the open window.

There was a police officer in North Bay Village, the little town that was part of my beat as a reporter for the *Miami Herald*, who warned me always to stay one car length behind the car in front of me. It would protect me from ambush, he said. He had once been investigated for minor wrongdoing, nothing

on the scale of the charges that landed his fellow cops in jail—
selling police protection to a drug smuggler who turned out to
be an FBI agent.

There was a marriage I admired for many years, that of a
young man and a young woman taking care of work and house
and children together. Somewhere along the way they turned
from each other, so that it is now a struggle for them to come
face to face.

There was a baby nuzzling my neck blindly, grown now
into the sturdy four-year-old who weaves on her brand-new
bike on a sunny Sunday morning—the gentle bumps of her
spine tapering down her bare brown back, the tag sticking out
of her Winnie-the-Pooh underwear—weaving unsteadily in
much the same way as, long ago, I wobbled on a nameless, battered bicycle in the dusty streets of a town named Fariman, the
desert sky darkening into twilight. Dayi Morteza ran behind
me with his steadying hand on the back of the bike, until at
last I was ready and he let go and stood watching as I learned
to fly, leaving him behind where he stood under the yellow
streetlights.

What connects these things, other than the fact that my
eyes witnessed them? What is the common thread in our lives,
other than memory, that filter composed of our accumulated
moments, which has me thinking, each time I see the sun set,
of a saffron sky?

I look at my daughter, noticing the gap where her front
tooth was knocked out when she was two, the well-cut chest-
nut hair cupping the back of her neck. The highlights in her
hair are still gold, a holdover from her toddler years, when her
hair went from dark brown to bronze. If I had met her when I
was myself a little girl, I would have looked in awe at this fasci-
nating, privileged creature from another world, the gold in her
hair all of a piece with her blue bike, both agleam with the allure of the untouchable West.

Opening Day is two weeks away. Baseball is coming to St. Petersburg at last. Neil wants to take Mina to a game.

In tenth-grade English, which I took as a sixth-grader, I struggled uselessly with a passage about baseball, an excerpt from a Hemingway novel. It contained phrases like "the World Series," which no dictionary could have ever explained to me.

Not back then.

Not in that lifetime.

March 18, 1998

TONIGHT is the last Wednesday of the year 1376. At 2:54 P.M. on Friday, spring will begin, and with it the Iranian New Year, celebrated thus since the kings ruled in Persepolis.

In the past, my celebrations have ranged from nonexistent to token. I have not kept the Iranian calendar since I was a girl of fifteen, living in Chapel Hill and waiting to go home to Iran.

But when Mina turned two, I changed my ways. Now we celebrate Charshanbeh-soori—"festive Wednesday"—bidding farewell to winter and the old year. We celebrate Norooz ("New Day") when the year changes. We mark Sizdah-bedar, the thirteenth day of the new year, banishing bad fortune in the time-honored way by throwing our *sabzeh*—the greens sprouted especially for Norooz—into flowing water.

My delight on these occasions is largely forced. It is hard enough to celebrate a holiday in isolation—holidays are a communal event, their symbolism gaining potency through the shared acknowledgment of a community. It is harder still in my household, where I am the only Iranian born and bred. Even with Neil's unfailing support, the holiday for me feels like putting on a play for an audience of one.

This year will be different. My sister and her husband, Ali, with their two-year-old daughter, Daria, arrive in late afternoon. My parents and an old school friend come tommorrow. This Saturday is the Norooz Recital. That night we'll go to one of two parties put on by the two Iranian cultural associations—feuding with each other, it is true—in Tampa Bay.

This year I can believe that Norooz for Mina carries some of the excitement that it held for me as a child. The new clothes, the presents, the family visits, the countdown as we gathered around the haft-sin. The haft-sin, the functional equivalent of the Christmas tree or the menorah, is a metaphor for life, a collection of symbolic objects laid out for the New Year. It must include at least seven (*haft*) items beginning with the letter *s* (*sin*). Greens and apples and Russian olives for abundance, gold coins for prosperity, hyacinth for beauty, vinegar and garlic for life's bitter moments. The haft-sin is usually accompanied by other symbolic items: painted eggs for fertility (some say the Easter egg originated with this old Persian tradition). The Koran for religion. A mirror that reflects the lit candles, symbolizing the future. The future is always unknown, often uncertain, so let us tip the odds in our favor by starting the year out sweet, with a taste of honey or a piece of baklava.

Tomorrow, I'll pick up the hyacinth I ordered from a local florist, the final touch for my haft-sin. Tonight we celebrate Festive Wednesday. We are supposed to attend a party at a nearby park, complete with the traditional year-end bonfires. But when I look up the directions, I find to my dismay that the party was last night. I'd forgotten about the tradition of celebrating holidays the night before.

We'll have to improvise. I pull out stacks of newspaper, a couple of metal pots, and a empty tin of Twinings Earl Grey tea. I shred newspaper into the containers and set them at a short distance from one another along the driveway. We gather the children outside just as the sky is beginning to darken. Not without trepidation, I hold a match to the first pile of newspaper.

The wind off the sea blows it out right away. It takes several tries to get the fires going, with Mina jumping up and down in excitement. In the misty twilight, with slate-colored clouds rolling in from Tampa Bay, the flames flicker brightly. They are a far cry from the roaring bonfires of my childhood, fed by tumbleweed brought in by the truckload from the desert and sprinkled with gasoline. Their flames leaped above my head so that we flung ourselves across in mingled terror and glee, our faces eerie in the fireglow, eyes and throat burning with smoke.

But there is fire, and there are children, and there is the familiar taste of smoke. A mizzling rain begins. The drops are cool on my face. I am seized by a spark of the old excitement, and when I jump over the little fires it is not entirely for the children's benefit. I chant the firesong: "My yellowness shall be yours. Your redness shall be mine." A trade of illness for health, the sallow skin of winter's end for the rosy heart of the fire. Mina and Daria watch, spellbound, delight mingling with fear in their eyes.

I jump again with Mina in my arms. She starts the chant, remembering pieces of it from last year, when we leaped over candles. Neil takes a turn. I stand in front of the house, shoulder to shoulder with Afsaneh. "Remember the bonfires in Iran, how high they were?" I say. "Yeah," she says, my nostalgia reflected in her eyes.

"You'd better hope no one calls the fire department," Ali says. "They won't," I answer. "It's such a tiny fire." But I look nervously around for neighbors, their eyes agog and their faces disapproving of this outlandish, pagan display.

Fortunately, however, the streets are deserted. The fires quickly dwindle to smoke and cinders. Mina screws up her courage and jumps over the tiny flame in the Twinings can. Daria holds her floppy-eared stuffed puppy tight and jumps once the flames are all gone, laughing gleefully.

In less than an hour it is over. "More Charshanbeh-soori," Mina says. I can't bear her disappointment or my own. "Wait here," I say. In the house, I grab a few pieces of crockery from the back of the kitchen cabinets. I bought them five years ago from the potters at Mend, just outside Gonabad. "Why are you weighting down your bags with this junk?" Khaleh Farah asked me at the time. "It's earth from Iran," I answered. She was silenced.

Khaleh Farah was right. The little vases and cups proved to be largely useless, until now. I bring them outside and instruct Mina to climb on top of Afsaneh and Ali's rented green compact. For my sister and me, it was the roof of our house in Tehran, but I suppose our children must pay the price of living in a well-regulated country. Daria sits next to Mina, and the girls' fathers stretch out an arm on either side of the children, just in case. The two take turns flinging the crockery, watching it break into pieces on the driveway. Another rite of closure. I remember the deep satisfaction I felt as a child when I flung my earthenware water jug from the roof and watched it shatter on the porch below, the damp stain spreading on the flagstones.

Mina still wants more. She asks Afsaneh and Ali if they can think of anything we've forgotten. She comes back to me asking if we have *ajil*, the traditional Charshanbeh-soori fruit-nut, sweet-salt mixture: pistachios, raisins, almonds, hazelnuts, dried mulberries, and crunchy, salty roast chickpeas. "I don't have any," I tell her with regret, wishing I had thought to order some. "Next year."

Mina settles for eating three Iranian raisin cookies imported from Toronto. The cookies are buttery and thin and crisp. Ali brews tea in the samovar. I carry a gallon jug of water outside, where Mina, supervised by Afsaneh, pours it into the pots, drowning the soot and ashes. In the cloudbank above, streaks of lightning briefly illuminate the driveway, helping

Ali and Neil sweep up the broken crockery. The sea is invisible now, but in the distance I can see the string of twinkling lights on the Sunshine Skyway, the bridge linking St. Petersburg to Sarasota.

It is a long way from Tehran. But for a few minutes tonight, standing with my sister in the firelit shadows, I barely felt the distance.

March 21, 1998

I HAD low expectations for this Norooz party, held in a Holiday Inn in downtown Tampa. Even so, I am impressed. In the entryway to the ballroom, the Iranian Cultural Association has arranged an elaborate haft-sin. An ice sculpture depicts the map of Iran. The well-heeled crowd sits at numbered tables, and the program opens with speechs and a proclamation from the office of Florida's governor, Lawton Chiles. Each table has a centerpiece of *sabzeh* at least five inches tall—far superior to the pale greens I sprouted at home. In one corner, images of Iran—the ancient ruins of Persepolis, museum artifacts from Susa, blue tiled mosques in Isfahan—are projected onto a white screen. Children wearing traditional dress are to receive prizes, and here and there a child is dressed in the colorful, flowing skirts of Iranian tribal women.

We have just started on our Greek salads when a tall, handsome man wearing a red bow tie and cummerbund stops by to welcome us. He has walnut skin and silver hair and speaks with my father in cultured tones, responding gracefully to our compliments. "Now if we can only inject our heritage into our children," he is saying to Baba, his hand resting on the back of my father's chair. Baba is nodding. This is the common lament of Iranians in exile. Moments later, it is vividly illustrated when a little girl in native dress goes up for a prize. The master of ceremonies asks her a question in Farsi, but she does not understand. "Well, at least she is wearing native dress," the emcee says with an awkward laugh.

A traditional quartet, sitting cross-legged on low cushions on the floor, plays classical Persian music during dinner. Eventually the sad, slow melodies yield to pop tunes on the stereo and children dance with exuberance on the postage-stamp-size dance floor. After dessert, there is a stir at the door. The tall man who welcomed us walks in with measured steps, dressed now in a gorgeous gold-embroidered red robe and trousers, wearing a flowing white beard and a tall brimless hat such as those common in nineteenth-century Iran. Amoo Norooz—Uncle Norooz—carries a bag of presents on one shoulder, and children immediately flock to him.

Mina follows him around the room for a long time after she has received her crisp two-dollar bill in a clean white envelope. Her eyes are wide and full of wonder. "Is Amoo Norooz real?" she asks me. I hesitate, then say, "No. He's an idea."

"Is this Amoo Norooz real?"

"No."

"So when will Amoo Norooz be real? I want the real one."

I fall back on what I call the Barney Alibi. "He is real—in your imagination. He lives in your imagination."

Mina is not satisfied. Neither am I.

April 1, 1998 (Farvardin 12, 1377)

M Y FRIEND Forough is going to Tehran on Saturday. I rush down to the outlet mall near Sarasota. After an hour in the dressing room of Westport Woman, I emerge with a cobalt blue outfit for my cousin Maryam and a red one for my cousin Soodi. This is no easy feat, finding long-sleeved clothes (short sleeves are not permitted in Iran in public) in Florida in Spring.

I call Forough to find out when I can bring by the clothes, which she will take to Iran for me. We make a date, then compare notes on Norooz parties. Forough and her husband, Ali, went to the one at the University of South Florida in Tampa— a less formal affair than the dinner my family and I chose to attend. "How was your party?" Forough wants to know. "I heard it was dreadful."

"I thought it was great," I tell her, surprised. "There were some problems with the mike and the dancing started too late for us, but I was impressed. So were my parents. They're used to pretty fancy parties in Toronto."

"I heard the *tar* player had a real attitude," Forough says, launching into the list of criticisms she heard from friends who attended our party. We keep talking, trying to reconcile these differing reports of the same event. We conclude that the problem is the tendency toward infighting that so often exists among exiles. I'm not sure what causes it, but suspect it has something to do with feeling threatened. I've noticed that groups under stress tend to pull apart—the losing side in a game of Pictionary, the passengers of the *Titanic*, the underclass in any society. Perhaps this is why the two Iranian cultural groups in Tampa Bay have devoted a fair bit of time, and a couple of mailings, to putting each other down.

Ali is trying to get the two groups to meet and work together, maybe even merge, Forough tells me. "I can't see it," I say. "Their styles are totally opposite. Besides, there's nothing wrong with having two groups, two events, two choices. If only they could get along."

"Well, everyone knows character assassination is an art among Iranians," Forough says.

Before we say good-bye, she asks me if I'm going to the Sizdah-bedar picnic. "The Sizdah-bedar picnic!" I say enthusiastically. "I'd like to go but I'm not sure. I'll have to talk to Neil."

I hang up the phone, vaguely ashamed. I know in my heart that we will not go to the picnic. Although our reasons vary from event to event, Neil and I rarely attend the picnics, concerts, and poetry nights sponsored by Iranians here.

Years ago, it dawned on me that just because someone was Iranian did not mean I had much in common with them. We have little enough leisure time as a family that we guard our weekends closely. But there is more to my reclusiveness.

Iranians in America, like many immigrants, are a troubled group. Take away the financial problems, language barriers, and emotional challenges of immigration, take away the political schisms that cause mutual distrust, and you are still left with the central dilemma of assimilation. The need to belong is a powerful thing. It pits those of us who are children of other worlds against ourselves and one another.

It made the Iranian clerk I encountered a few years ago at Bloomingdale's, in Rockville, Maryland, stare coldly when I spoke to her in Farsi. She rang up my sale without a word. A few months later, when an Iranian handed me the numbered tag I took into the dressing room of another department store, I was careful to thank her in English. I pretended that I did not recognize the almond skin, arched eyebrows, and glossy hair of a countrywoman.

A memory surfaces, one I haven't summoned in years. I am twenty-something, working at the *Miami Herald*. I fly up to Washington, D.C., to get a new passport. I stay at the Kalorama Guesthouse, near the zoo, and wake early in the morning to go to the Iranian Interests Section on Wisconsin Avenue. The Interests Section requires that applicants wear Islamic dress. Waiting on the steps of the guesthouse for a cab, I am painfully conscious of the scarf on my head. I try to catch the eyes of people passing by, hungry for an opportunity to show them that, despite my appearance, I am not one of *them*. Let me speak a sentence loaded with colloquialisms. See, I am fluent in

English! I have no accent! I'm like *you*. Don't consign me to the trash heap, where the unforgivably different belong. Don't look at me as if I were an animal at the zoo, an object of curiosity and spurious compassion.

This inner dialogue fills me with shame, yet I am helpless against it. I have become a party to my own disenfranchisement. The worst part of being told in a thousand ways, subtle and not, that one is inferior is the way that message worms itself into the heart. It is not enough to battle the prejudice of others, one must also battle the infection within.

I have struggled for years with my own ambivalence. Socializing with other Iranians invokes my angst in painful ways. Yet despite my discomfort, in every city I have lived I have sought out my countrymen and tried to establish meaningful connections with them.

Only in St. Petersburg, with our children as a common bond, have I succeeded. Only in Iran—or in Toronto, where relationships are cemented by family ties—is it easy to be with other Iranians. My closest friends, including my husband, are American.

Sometimes I get tired of the struggle.

So it is that each year I go to great lengths to travel to Iran. Each week I spend hours preparing our Farsi lesson.

Yet I won't make the effort to go to a picnic half an hour away in Clearwater.

April 2, 1998

WE WAIT for Neil to get home from work before setting out. It is Sizdah-bedar, the thirteenth of the year. Our family won't be going to the picnic, but we will walk to the beach and cast our *sabzeh* on running waters, to take the ill omen out of the day.

The children double up in the stroller, Mina holding two

tiny saucers of the pale, etiolated stalks I sprouted from lentils. The big plate, the family *sabzeh*, is in the wagon. I can't wait to get rid of it; after nearly a month, it is buggy as well as scraggly.

We walk toward Fourteenth Street under a new moon. At the little park on the water, Mina stands on the concrete ledge of the bait pool, dancing with excitement. "I want to throw it in," she says about fifty times.

I show her how to grab the stalks so the whole *sabzeh* comes up in her hand, a pale hank illuminated by the streetlights. As it lands with a splash in the shallow water, I call out "Goodbye to bad luck for Max, good-bye to bad luck for Mina, good-bye to bad luck for all of us."

The *sabzeh* doesn't go anywhere, floating in the still pool, a pale circle against the fluid darkness. I look at it pensively, thinking of the rushing streams and rivers of childhood Sizdah-bedars, the green tufts of *sabzeh* bobbing in the water that swept it away. It will go out with the tide, I assure myself. The tradition will have been honored. This is what matters to me, not the thought of a year's worth of bad luck floating in the bait pool at our doorstep.

As we walk back, I listen to Mina chattering. Each time she throws an English word into the Farsi she is directing my way, I cringe inwardly. This is the first year of her life that has passed without a trip to Iran. Her English has been seeping into her Farsi for a couple of months now. I think of wells and salt-water intrusion. I think of holes in a dike.

She goes to preschool five mornings a week. At home she has a sitter, and Neil, and television. The English words are pouring into her agile mind from every direction. They are simply more accessible, crowding out Farsi words that more rarely see the light of day. I remember interviewing an Iranian scholar once, before I had children, and asking if his six-year-old spoke Farsi. "No," he said. "The dominant culture is simply too dominant."

Anxiety seizes me, for I know that language is the lifeblood of culture. Language is the self, reflected and clothed in nouns and verbs and adjectives. Without Farsi, the Iranian in Mina will shrivel up and die. Even as I think this, I know that my greatest fear is of my own inner shriveling, not Mina's. In guarding Mina's heritage, I guard my own, for they are linked. My daughter, this piping voice in my house speaking the words I learned at my mother's knee, is a lifeline to my first self. When Neil and I go away together and I am deprived of this link for a few days, I feel building in me the sense of disconnection and loss that characterized the years before her birth. I feel like a beached whale, slowly drying up.

Language, I remind myself, is fluid. What is lost can be regained. This time next year, when we go back to Iran, it will be the English words that take a back seat. Bilingualism, like biculturalism, is a seesaw.

Nonetheless, to make sure the seesaw does not descend too far, I start fining her for every English word that surfaces in a Farsi sentence.

Soon, the jar of pennies I hand her in the morning to pay her fines becomes obsolete. Mina develops the habit of sticking to one language or the other.

I have plugged the holes in the dike.

September 1998

MAX IS one year old. His hair is a mixture of gold and red, with fine spun-silver strands around the temples. A recessive gene on Neil's side, we think, shaking our heads at this blond child of two dark-haired parents. His hands are surprisingly strong. When I pick him up, he braces those hands against my chest and pushes himself away. Having found his vantage point, he rests in my embrace, peering at me intently, looking at my face, into my eyes.

Starting to figure out where I end and he begins.

I am like Max, I think to myself. I push away from that which I love the most—my family and my culture—while holding on to it. When my parents left for Canada, I stayed behind. I chose to love an American, finding in our marriage a safe vantage point from which I could embrace my heritage without losing myself in its dark corners.

All my adult life I have created distance, and distance brings me grief. Yet distance has also brought perspective. Distance has allowed me to make peace with myself and my heritage. It has allowed me to attempt to forge a life that is true to both my cultures, both my selves.

This is America's true gift to me, its greatest opportunity.

IT IS a starry night. The Big Dipper hangs high above us as we set out for our walk. Mina sits behind Max in the stroller made for one, her legs extending on either side of the baby. When Max moves, his sister laughs in delight. "He tickled my foot," she says.

The neighborhood is silent, lamplight and the occasional blue blur of a television set shining through closed windows. A cool wind tosses the heads of the palm trees and makes the oak leaves rustle. My mind, still wound up from the day, searches for occupation as I push the stroller. I start singing "Ey Eeran," the anthem we sang at our Norooz program.

Though the words are familiar to me from childhood, I have never learned them by heart. In school we were expected to memorize "Long Live Our King of Kings." Even so, my mind reaches for the words and they are there, one after the other forming on my tongue. I feel the same thrill that comes when leaping across stepping-stones, landing firmly on one after the other when you know that each moment you might slip and fall.

I sing the stanzas I know once, twice, three times. Mina, annoyed, tells me to stop. I think she suspects my motives in singing the song. Like most children, she wants to own her learning. But I wonder uneasily if there is another reason, if she is developing an aversion to things Iranian. I worry that my own ambivalence is contagious, that it leaks out of my eyes, giving the lie to the robust confidence I project.

As we approach the water, I see the lights of the Sunshine Skyway suspended in the darkness where sea meets sky. I stand by the water for long moments, turning my face to the sea breeze, asking it to sweep away my sadness. We spent last month with my family in Toronto, and as always after such visits, living in this island of our own making feels unutterably lonely.

Walking back, we search the shadows for Neil, hoping he is home from work and has headed out to meet us. A figure, white shirt gleaming, emerges from the darkness. He passes into the yellow glow of a streetlight and we call out glad greetings. Soon, Neil is pushing the stroller. I walk beside him, absently humming "Ey Eeran."

"*Maman*, sing it again," Mina says.

I look at her hopefully. "I thought you were tired of it."

"Sing it again," Mina repeats.

We walk up to the house, still singing. The roof is outlined against the starry sky, the windows dark. The flower basket hanging to the side of the porch sways, red and white impatiens nodding in the breeze.

The empty house, our song, the bright flowers—all speak to me of my choices in life.

There is emptiness, yes, and it echoes.

But there is also space, and sometimes we are able to fill it with our own music.

Epilogue

St. Petersburg
January 5, 1999

KHALEH Farah has found us the perfect apartment in Mashad. Three bedrooms, furnished, with a washing machine and a dishwasher. "But make sure to bring your own dishwashing powder," she says. "He says the powders here are no good."

"Does it have a *farangi* toilet?" I ask.

"I don't know," she says. "I'll find out."

We discuss dates for my family's Tehran–Mashad tickets, which will be hard to get; the holy city is a popular destination during the Norooz holiday. This year, God willing, we will celebrate the New Year in Mashad. This year, the Iranian government willing, we will spend all spring and part of the summer in Iran. This year, with four months of study behind him, Neil will speak my language at last.

"What will you do if Neil doesn't get a visa?" Khaleh Farah asks.

"I don't know," I say, anxiety knotting my stomach. "I called today. He has to get a visa."

I tell her I'll call next week and hang up. As I drive to work, my head is spinning with plans and strategies for the trip.

In the next few weeks, my everyday routines are subsumed by a parallel parade of telephone calls and faxes, forms and passport photos, airline and hotel reservations. As the logistician for Operation Four Months In Iran, I am forced to wake Neil up at 1 A.M. to go to his office, where he has left documents that must be faxed instantly to the Ministry of Foreign Affairs in Tehran. Another night I go to bed exhausted as soon as the children are settled and set my clock for 11:30 P.M. —8 A.M. Tehran time. "Call back next week," the precise-sounding man on the other end of the line tells me after I have completed another round of bureaucratic exchanges in order to get him the information he needs to find Neil's file. By the time I crawl back into bed at two o'clock, I find it impossible to sleep.

I lie there in the darkness, my thoughts and stomach churning, staring at the cedar ceiling with absurd longing. I want to hold on to that ceiling, to these walls around me, to the streets that I drive when I drop Mina off at her preschool. I want to pump my gas at the Amoco on the corner. I want to have cashew butter and jelly sandwiches and Perrier for lunch.

But I know the time has come to tear myself away from my moorings once again, to reclaim my other country, my other life.

Everything in me resists what is about to come. When friends comment on how exciting this venture is, I smile an empty smile, wishing things were that simple. I feel like a vessel on a turbulent river, my ears filled with the thunder of the approaching falls. I do not want to go over the edge. I do not want to reopen the seams of my life and my heart, to revisit the pain of leaving Iran for America.

Yet there can be no backpaddling. For to put the heartache behind me is to be sundered from what I love.

Acknowledgments

I wish to thank my wise and loving friend Deb Kollars, for giving me a kick in the pants when I needed it most, back when this book was a distant dream and I didn't know how to go about making it a reality.

I thank my parents, Homa Ghassemi and Khalil Asayesh, who have taught me about courage, who have taught me about heart, and who showed both qualities when they made the choice to accompany us abroad. Thanks to Homajoon and Baba, I was never wholly adrift.

I thank my father and my sister, Afsaneh Asayesh, for their valuable contributions during the editing of the manuscript. In Iran, Afzal Vosooghi read my work and made many helpful suggestions. All three devoted time and thought to this process despite their hectic lives. Afsaneh's support for this book has been especially precious to me.

My parents made no effort to censor my work, even when it ventured into painful topics. For this act of love, trust, and forbearance, I am more grateful than I can say.

I am grateful to my extended family in Iran and Toronto for suffering my intrusions into their stories in the process of telling mine. I am especially grateful for my *khalehs* and for Ammeh, whose love and presence sustain and nourish me, no matter how far away they are. My loving thanks to Dayi Abbas for his support during our early years in America. I am grateful for my brothers of the heart, Reza and Mehra, who know what it is to claim new identities at the expense of the old.

This book is for them and for all of us who inhabit the difficult places in between cultures.

Deanne Urmy has been the editor of my dreams—intuitive, incisive and caring, gifted with humor and common sense. Her encouragement and understanding sustained me as I struggled with the challenge of writing a book during an intense time in the life of any family—the birth of a child. From the first, she understood what I was trying to accomplish.

I thank my agent, Deborah Grosvenor, for believing in my work and helping me select Beacon Press as my publisher.

Andrew Barnes and Paul Tash of the *St. Petersburg Times* lead an extraordinary institution, a place that combines excellence with humanity. Their caring, sense of balance and respect for individuals and the families they are a part of has made a difference to our family.

I was fortunate in the generosity of George Rahdert, who offered me a space to work when I desperately needed it, granting me that rarest of all commodities—peace and quiet. I thank Deborah Brook and the rest of his staff for making me welcome.

My deepest thanks to the women who cared for my children in this period, allowing me to go off, confident of their wellbeing. Avery Woodworth provided a dream summer at a crucial juncture; Tracey Curl providentially appeared when

Avery left for Germany. Alice Carlson, Heather Dowling, Cyndi Child, and Lisa Fink helped bridge the gaps. Alice Tomascewski has always been there for us.

My mother-in-law, Gloria Polonsky, did not let the fact that she lives in faraway Las Vegas prevent her from responding to my occasional SOS. Thank you, Glorious Gloria.

Many thanks to Roxann Beidler for being there.

I am grateful to my friend Rita Blanton, who helped me shape an American identity with pathways to the past.

I am grateful to my children, Mina and Max, who ground me and fill my life with meaning.

I am grateful to Neil, a busy—and brilliant—newspaper editor who manages to find time for his family no matter what news is breaking, a companion of the road who always goes the distance. *Rafigh-e-nimeh-rah nisti.*

Author's Note

THIS is a work of nonfiction. However, I have deemed it prudent to use assumed names throughout the manuscript wherever potentially controversial issues are addressed or personal privacy is at stake. In the interests of organization, I have also made minor changes in the chronology of events in a few instances, where doing so did not compromise the essence of the anecdote.